ST GERMANUS OF CONSTANTINOPLE
ON
THE DIVINE LITURGY

ON THE DIVINE LITURGY

GERMANUS OF CONSTANTINOPLE

*The Greek Text with
Translation, Introduction and Commentary
by*
PAUL MEYENDORFF

ST VLADIMIR'S SEMINARY PRESS
CRESTWOOD, NEW YORK 10707
1999

Library of Congress Cataloging-in-Publication Data

Germanus I, St, Patriarch of Constantinople, d. ca. 733.
    On the divine liturgy.

    Includes bibliographical references.
    1. Lord's Supper—Orthodox Eastern Church—Liturgy.   2. Lord's
Supper—Catholic Church—Liturgy.   3. Orthodox Eastern Church—
Liturgy.   4. Catholic Church—Byzantine rite—Liturgy.   I. Meyendorff,
Paul.   II. Title.
BX375.E7504713   1984   264'.019   84-27615
ISBN 0-88141-038-1

ON THE DIVINE LITURGY

Translation Copyright © 1984
ST VLADIMIR'S SEMINARY PRESS
575 Scarsdale Rd., Crestwood, NY 10707
1-800-204-2665

ISBN 0-88141-038-1

PRINTED IN THE UNITED STATES OF AMERICA

264.019
Ger

ACKNOWLEDGEMENTS

This translation was originally undertaken in the context of a reading course on Byzantine liturgical commentaries at the University of Notre Dame, South Bend, Indiana. I wish particularly to thank Professor Robert Taft, SJ, of Notre Dame, who first suggested the project and without whose assistance and encouragement it would never have been completed. I am also grateful to William J. Churchill, Ph.D. and to the Rev. James Jorgenson, Ph.D., who read the final draft and suggested corrections and changes. Any errors or inaccuracies which remain are strictly my own.

CONTENTS

INTRODUCTION

The eighth-century commentary on the liturgy by St Germanus (†733), Patriarch of Constantinople from 715 to 730, remains little known today. This is despite the fact that it exercised tremendous influence in the Byzantine Christian world from the time of its composition at least to the time of Cabasilas' work in the fourteenth century. It was included, along with the text of the liturgies of John Chrysostom and Basil, in the first printed edition of the Byzantine liturgy.[1] It was also influential in Russia, where it was included in manuscripts of the liturgy from the thirteenth century, as well as in the *Sluzhba Tolkovaia*, or "Liturgy commented," and even in some editions of the Slavonic service book, or *Sluzhebnik*.[2] Numerous manuscripts of the commentary are extant, and this is further evidence of its popularity and broad diffusion.[3] Even so,

---

[1] D. Doucas, Αἱ Θεῖαι λειτουργίαι τοῦ ἁγίου Ἰωάννου τοῦ Χρυσοστόμου, Βασιλείου τοῦ Μεγάλου, καὶ ἡ τῶν Προηγιασμένων, Γερμανοῦ ἀρχιεπισκόπου Κωνσταντινουπόλεως ἱστορία ἐκκλησιαστικὴ καὶ μυστικὴ θεωρία (Rome, 1526).

[2] R. Taft, "The Liturgy of the Great Church: an Initial Synthesis of Structure and Interpretation on the Eve of Iconoclasm," *Dumbarton Oaks Papers* 34-35 (1980-1981) 46. Henceforth referred to as Taft, "The Liturgy of the Great Church."

[3] These are catalogued in F. E. Brightman, "The *Historia Mystagogica* and Other Greek Commentaries on the Byzantine Liturgy," *Journal of Theological Studies* 9 (1908) 248-257; and a more recent analysis can be found in R. Bornert, *Les commentaires byzantins de la divine liturgie du VIIe au XVe siècle* (= *Archives de l'Orient chrétien* 9) (Paris: Institut français d'études byzantines,

the work remains inaccessible to the modern reader, the only modern-language translation being in Russian.[4] It is to fill this void that the present translation is being offered.

The *Historia Ecclesiastica* was for centuries the quasi-official explanation of the Divine Liturgy for the Byzantines. At first glance, it appears to be only one of those numerous "allegorical" documents which are not held in the highest regard by theologians today.[5] Yet this document is of interest for historical purposes, for it shows how the Byzantines understood the liturgy for the greater part of their history. Moreover, the commentary appears at a time of great flux in the life of the Byzantine church, at the outbreak of the great iconoclastic controversies, a period which marked a strong shift in theology and piety. Seen in this context, the document is revealed also as a *theological* statement. In fact, it is only in this context that Germanus' commentary can be properly read and understood. Without this perspective, the text appears highly confusing, composed as it is of overlapping, and at times mutually contradictory, levels of symbolism.

In this introduction, we shall attempt to place the *Historia Ecclesiastica* in its proper historical and theological context. In doing so, we shall generally be following the research and conclusions of Bornert and Taft, both leading scholars in the field of Byzantine liturgy.[6] We shall also give a brief description of the shape of the liturgy commented on by Germanus. Chiefly, however, we shall deal with the background to the commentary, with the literary genre and style, and particularly its antecedents in the

---

1966) 130-145. Henceforth referred to as Bornert, *Les commentaires byzantins.*

[4]N. Krasnosel'tsev, *Svedenia o nekotorykh liturgicheskikh rukopisiakh vatikanskoi biblioteki* (Kazan', 1885) 323-375.

[5]As indicated by Taft, "The Liturgy of the Great Church," 45.

[6]Cited above, notes 2 and 3.

works of Pseudo-Dionysius, Maximus the Confessor, and Theodore of Mopsuestia. Finally, we shall attempt to show how Germanus fits into this tradition, and his own contribution to it.

As this translation is being published in a popular patristic series, aimed at the general audience, this introduction cannot include a discussion of such important issues as Germanus' style, vocabulary, choice of words, as well as the difficulties inherent in the translation of an 8th c. Byzantine text. These could well be the subject of a future, scholarly essay. Suffice it to say that, in this translation, an effort has been made to render the meaning of the Greek text as literally as possible—though this does at times render injustice to the English language.

THE TEXT

The present translation is based on the Greek text of Germanus' commentary as reconstructed by N. Borgia: this text is reproduced facing the English translation.[7] Borgia's edition is based chiefly on two manuscripts, *Vaticanus graecus* 790 and *Neapolitanus graecus* 63, and also includes the Latin version of Anastasius the Librarian, a translation of the commentary which dates to 869-870.[8] The Latin version, only a century later than the original, served as the guide for the reconstruction. Borgia's edition is close

---

[7] *Il commentario liturgico di S. Germano patriarca Constantinopolitano e versiona latina di Anastasio Bibliotecario* (= *Studi Liturgici* 1) (Grottaferrata, 1912).

[8] Bornert, *Les commentaires byzantins,* 128. The Latin text has been reconstructed by S. Petrides, based on 9-10th cent. mss., in "Traités liturgiques de Saint Maxime et de Saint Germain, traduits par Anastase le bibliothecaire," *Revue de l'Orient Chrétien* 10 (1905) 287-309.

to that published by Krasnosel'tsev in 1885, which is based on *Codex* 327 of the Moscow Synodal Library.[9] The text of Germanus published by Migne is a corrupt medieval text.[10]

Vat. gr. 790, a manuscript of the 14-15th century, transmits what scholars believe is the shortest and most primitive version of the text. It is identical to that given in Moscow Synodal Library *Codex* 327, which dates to the 16th cent. Only two passages in this manuscript appear to be interpolations: the chapter on the symbolism of the simandron (ch 2) and the commentary on the Lord's Prayer (ch 42).[11] This text is reproduced in standard-size print in the present edition.

Neap. gr. 63, a manuscript dating to 1526, contains interpolations added to the text by the 9th century, when it was translated into Latin by Anastasius. These interpolations, indented in this edition, are as follows:[12]

1. Chapters 17, 15, and 18 of the *Mystagogy* of Maximus the Confessor are inserted into ch 41 of Germanus;

2. Extracts of the *Letters* I, 136, 122, 228 of Isidore of Peluza are added;

3. A new chapter on the prothesis is added into ch 22, new sections are added to chapters dealing with the Trisagion (ch 25) and the censing before the gospel (ch 30); these contrast sharply with the form and content of the original commentary;

4. A long description of the monastic habit is added (ch 19).

---

[9]Bornert, *Les commentaires byzantins,* 128.

[10]PG 98, 384-453.

[11]Bornert, *Les commentaires byzantins,* 130-131.

[12]Bornert, *Les commentaires byzantins,* 136-137.

In addition, the text enclosed in brackets comes from different manuscripts and fills in gaps in the Greek text, thus making it correspond to Anastasius' Latin translation. In short, Borgia has reconstructed a Greek text to correspond to Anastasius' version of the ninth century, and has indicated as well the primitive form of the commentary.

The tremendous variety in the manuscripts of Germanus' commentary is the result of its great popularity and wide distribution, and its acceptance as the quasi-official explanation of the Byzantine liturgy. During the centuries following the work's composition, however, the liturgy itself continued to grow and evolve. These changes led to the many interpolations to the text, as well as to alterations in its internal order. Thus, at a date later than Anastasius, the passages explaining the *proskomede,* or rite of preparation of the gifts, were moved from their original place immediately before the transfer of gifts, to a new position, before the liturgy.[13]

Further, the authoritative position of the commentary in Byzantine theology led to its ascription to various persons, including Patriarchs Germanus II,[14] Germanus III,[15] and even Basil the Great,[16] and Cyril of Jerusalem.[17] Borgia, however, strongly affirms the authorship of Germanus I, relying heavily on the witness of Anastasius and on the state of the liturgy which the commentary describes.[18] This

---

[13]Bornert, *Les commentaires byzantins,* 139.

[14]Bornert, *Les commentaires byzantins,* 126. He was patriarch from 1220 to 1240.

[15]Bornert, *Les commentaires byzantins,* 127. Patriarch from 1265 to 1266.

[16]Brightman, "The *Historia Mystagogica,*" 250. Brightman doubts the authorship of Germanus.

[17]Bornert, *Les commentaires byzantins,* 127.

[18] N. Borgia, *"La* Ἐξήγησις *di S. Germano e la versione latina di Anastasio Bibliotecario," Roma e l'Oriente* 2 (1911) 144-156, 219-228, 286-296, 346-354.

conclusion is now generally accepted by modern scholars.[19]

THE AUTHOR

Germanus was born some time between 630 and 650: it is not possible to fix the date precisely, though the early 640's seems most likely.[20] He was a Byzantine of noble lineage—his father was a relative of the Emperor Heraclius, and held high office during his reign, but was subsequently implicated in the assassination of the Emperor Constans and was put to death by order of Constans' son, Constantine IV (668-685). In connection with this affair, Germanus is said to have been castrated, although he was apparently allowed to keep the family property.[21] These factors led Germanus to seek a career in the church. Thus, from the beginning of Constantine's reign, Germanus joined the ranks of the clergy attached to the cathedral church in Constantinople, Hagia Sophia.

An educated man, Germanus took an active part in church life. He had a leading role in the Sixth Ecumenical Council (680-681), which condemned monothelitism (the teaching that Christ had only one—divine—will). Some time later, he was appointed Metropolitan of Cyzicus, a see under the jurisdiction of Constantinople. He was famous as a preacher, teacher, and interpreter of scripture, and was active in ecclesiastical and political affairs. Thus, in 715, already an aged man, he was elected Patriarch of

---

[19]Bornert, *Les commentaires byzantins,* 128; R. Taft, *The Great Entrance* (= *Orientalia Christiana Analecta* 200) (Rome, 1978) xxxviii.

[20]C. Garton and L. Westerink, *Germanos on Predestined Terms of Life* (= *Arethusa Monographs* VII) (Buffalo, NY: SUNY, 1979) v-vi.

[21]Garton, *Germanos,* vi-vii.

Constantinople, a position he held for fifteen years until
his deposition by the iconoclastic Emperor Leo III. He died
a few years later, in 733.

It was during Germanus' patriarchate that the first
iconoclastic crisis broke out. This was caused by a number
of factors which converged in this period. First, the mono-
physites, who affirmed that Christ had only one, divine
nature, emphasized Christ's divinity to the detriment of the
incarnation—this naturally led to their dislike for any
depiction of Christ as a man. Second, the Paulicians,
strongly influenced by Manicheism, held all matter to be
evil, and this belief led to their rejection of material images.
Contact with Islam, which also rejected all images, was
an additional factor, both for polemical and catechetical
reasons. The determining element, however, was the adoption and promotion of iconoclasm by the emperors. The
first major crisis took place when, in 725, Emperor Leo
issued an edict outlawing icons and ordering their destruc-
tion. Germanus refused to obey, and openly and strongly
maintained the orthodoxy of icons. In 730, a council composed of secular and ecclesiastical authorities loyal to the
emperor deposed Germanus and appointed Anastasius, an
iconoclast, as his successor.

In addition to the present commentary on the liturgy,
Germanus' chief writings include *On Heresies and Synods,*[22]
a historical work about the six Ecumenical Councils held
to that date. A number of other works are lost, including
the *Antapodotikos,* known to us from Photius, which dealt
with Origen's doctrine of universal salvation (*apokatastasis*).
A number of sermons, letters, liturgical hymns, and poems
survive, mostly in manuscript form, but their ascription to
Germanus is often uncertain.

Germanus died in 733 at his family estate in Platonion.
He was anathematized by the iconoclastic Council of 754,

[22]PG 98, 39-88.

but with the restoration of icons and the triumph of Orthodoxy in 787, he was rehabilitated and eventually canonized,
his feast day being celebrated on May 12.

THE LITURGY OF GERMANUS' TIME

We begin with a brief description of the liturgy as it
was celebrated in Constantinople in the eighth century.
We must be able to visualize the liturgy Germanus is describing to understand properly what he says, for it is
chiefly the *visual* aspects of the rite which he explains. And
the visual aspects of the Byzantine liturgy in Hagia Sophia,
the cathedral church of the capital city of the empire, were
impressive. It is precisely this strong visual effect, rather
than any rational discourse, which caused Vladimir's
emissaries (from Russia to Constantinople, A.D. 987) to
report: ". . . We knew not whether we were in heaven
or on earth. For on earth there is no such beauty, and
we are at a loss how to describe it. We only know that
God dwells there among men . . ."[23]

The edifice itself, built under Justinian and dedicated
in 537, is indeed hard to describe.

In sheer size it is one of the largest man-made
structures in the world; its great vaulted nave
easily surpasses all the vaulted interiors of antiquity
and the Middle Ages for space enclosed within a
single clear span. In engineering it is as puzzling
today as it was terrifying to Procopius, to whom it
appeared to soar aloft without reliable support,
theatening the safety of those within.[24]

[23]S. H. Cross and O. P. Sherbowitz-Wetzor, *The Russian Primary
Chronicle, Laurentian Text* (Cambridge, MS, 1953) 110-111.
[24]T. Mathews, *The Byzantine Churches of Istanbul. A Photo-*

Most striking about the church were the tremendous size of the nave, or body of the church, and the brilliance of its lighting.[25] Some thirty-five doors allowed easy access to the church, a feature absolutely necessary for a liturgy which was essentially stational, composed of numerous processions which were not restricted, as today, to a confined space, but encompassed the whole city in their rounds.

At the center of the nave, almost directly under the dome, stood the ambo, a large, oval platform with stairways leading up to it on both the east and west ends. Under the ambo, which was supported by eight large columns, was a space where the cantors stood. The ambo was connected to the sanctuary area by a long path, called the solea, with a barrier on either side. The sanctuary area was π-shaped, extending well into the nave, with chancel barriers (the precursor of our modern iconostasis) which were about waist-high. The altar table stood in front of the apse, which was completely filled with the synthronon, a series of semi-circular steps on which the clergy sat during the readings and homilies.[26]

The following is a description of the liturgy of Germanus' period:

A. *The Preparatory Rites*

These took place in the skeuophylakion, a circular structure located just to the north-east of Hagia Sophia. This building served as the treasury, where the liturgical

---

graphic Survey (University Park and London: Pennsylvania State University Press, 1976) 263. The most accessible study of Hagia Sophia and its liturgy is by the same author, *The Early Churches of Constantinople: Architecture and Liturgy* (University Park and London: Pennsylvania State University Press, 1971).

[25]Taft, "The Liturgy of the Great Church," 48.

[26]Mathews, *The Early Churches,* 96-99.

vessels were kept. Here the clergy vested for the services.
Here also the people brought their gifts before the beginning of the liturgy. There was as yet no formal "rite" of
preparation: the deacons simply selected bread and wine
from among the gifts brought by the people, and prepared
all the necessary implements, patens, chalices, etc.[27] In our
interpolated text, however, we can already detect the
development of today's prothesis rite.

On many days, there would be a station. Clergy and
people would gather at some place in the city, a church or
another site, for a service of prayer and intercession. Then
all would process to an intermediate station or to the
cathedral to the singing of antiphons. Antiphons consisted
of psalms sung by one or more psalmists, with short re-
frains, called troparia, sung by all the people. Arriving
at the atrium, a large courtyard in front of the church, the
people stopped while the clergy entered the narthex and
stood before the "royal doors" (reserved for the emperor
and clergy), which led from the narthex into the nave.
Here, they recited the Entrance (Introit) Prayer, and
then they processed into the church, while the assembled
people entered through all the other doors.

B. *The Enarxis*

This was a short office of three antiphons used on those
days when there was no station. It consisted of three psalms,
sung antiphonally, each preceded by a diaconal invitation,
"Let us pray to the Lord," and a prayer recited by one of
the priests. There was no opening doxology or "Litany
of Peace" at this point in the service. The patriarch was
not yet in church, but was vesting in his palace nearby.

---

[27]In our reconstruction, we are essentially repeating that offered
by Taft, "The Liturgy of the Great Church," 49ff.

The faithful gradually entered the church through its many doors, first dropping off their offerings at the skeuphylakion.

C. *The Introit*

This was the real beginning of the liturgy, everything prior being merely preparatory. The patriarch, already fully vested, arrived before the royal doors in the narthex and recited the Introit Prayer during the singing of the third antiphon, which normally consisted of Ps 94 (LXX), with the troparion "Only-begotten Son" (*Ho Monogenes*) as its final refrain. The text of the Introit Prayer is not the same as that of the present entrance prayer: "O Lord and master, our God, who in heaven has established the order and armies of angels and archangels to minister unto your majesty, grant that the holy angels may enter with us, and with us serve and glorify your goodness. . . ."[28] Then, preceded by the Gospel Book and the Cross, the procession entered the church. Germanus, in ch 24, sees this entrance as the coming upon earth of Christ himself: " 'Come let us worship and fall down before him: save us o Son of God.' And we proclaim the coming which was revealed to us in the grace of Jesus Christ." The singing of the Trisagion follows immediately, while the patriarch continues in procession around the ambo, up the solea, into the sanctuary, where he venerates the altar, then up to his throne (the "synthronon") in the back of the apse. We can still observe this last part of the procession at the present-day hierarchical liturgy.

---

[28]As translated by Taft, "The Liturgy of the Great Church," 51. The original Greek text, which appears in the earliest extant euchology, Barberini 336 (ca. 795), can be found in F. E. Brightman, *Liturgies Eastern and Western* (Oxford: Clarendon Press, 1896) 312.

D. *The Liturgy of the Word*

The patriarch, after entering the church in splendid procession, turns and greets the people: "Peace to all." Then he sits down and the readings begin. The prokeimenon precedes the epistle reading, and the alleluia psalm comes between epistle and Gospel. Germanus here again stresses the presence of Christ, Who comes to us in His word. The readings are proclaimed from the ambo in the center of the church. During the alleluia psalm, the Gospel book, which was placed on the altar table at the Introit, is incensed. A sermon follows the Gospel.

E. *The Great Entrance*

After the sermon, the patriarch and the clergy descend from the synthronon and stand around the altar. One of the deacons goes to the ambo to recite the petitions for the catechumens and their dismissal—this, by the time of Germanus, was already a mere formality.[29] The eiliton, a large veil, is spread over the altar. As one of the deacons continues the intercessions, several others, taking a censer, leave the church through one of the north-east doors, and go to the skeuophylakion. Completing the preparation of the gifts, they begin the procession back to the church, entering through one of the side doors directly across from the ambo. As they enter, the deacons begin to sing the Cherubic Hymn, which is then taken up by the psalmists.

Visually, the Great Entrance was the most dramatic rite in the liturgy. A pair of deacons led the procession with candles and incense. Next came a deacon with the flabellum, or fan, followed by deacons carrying the veils used to cover the chalices and patens. Then came the gifts themselves

---

[29]Taft, "The Liturgy of the Great Church," 53.

(the bread and wine to be consecrated), contained in the chalices and patens, and finally the aer, which was used to cover all the gifts. The procession moved from the side door to the center of the nave, just behind the ambo. If the emperor was present at the liturgy, he would meet the procession here, accompanied by his entire retinue. Doubled in size, the procession wound its way around the ambo and up along the solea to the doors of the sanctuary. There, the gifts were presented to the patriarch, and all the participants in the procession returned to their proper places.[30] No additional formulae accompanied the rite—there were no commemorations to interrupt the Cherubic Hymn, nor was anything said as the gifts were placed on the altar.[31]

As the psalmists completed the final repetition of the Cherubic Hymn, the patriarch bowed to his concelebrants around the altar and asked for their prayers. They responded with the text from Lk 1:35: "May the Holy Spirit come down upon you, and the power of the Most High overshadow you." Then the patriarch moved up to the altar for the anaphora, beginning with the preparatory Prayer of the Proskomede. No litany followed the Entrance.

F. *The Anaphora*

After completing his prayer, the patriarch turns to

---

[30]As reconstructed by Mathews, *The Early Churches,* 161-162.

[31]Taft, "The Liturgy of the Great Church," 53-54. The commemorations did not appear until medieval times, and the deposition formulae appeared only in the 13-14th centuries, under the influence of an increasingly allegorical approach to the liturgy. A complete description of the origin and development of the Great Entrance and its subsidiary rites is the classic work in English by Taft, *The Great Entrance.*

the people and says "Peace to all." The archdeacon then commands the assembled faithful to share the peace: "Let us love one another." All then exchange the kiss of peace with those of their own rank—clergy with clergy, lay people with lay, men with men, women with women. The only response to the diaconal command is the exchange of the kiss. Then all chant the Creed. The great veil, or aer, is removed from the gifts in preparation for the anaphora proper. The anaphora was said silently,[32] with no ceremonial action, and thus Germanus does not give it any sort of symbolic explanation. Rather, he gives a straightforward outline of the content of the prayer, which, on a normal Sunday in Constantinople, was that of St Basil.

G. *Lord's Prayer and Communion*

The Lord's Prayer followed the anaphora immediately, and then the distribution of communion. Germanus says little about either and ends his commentary rather abruptly. Perhaps this was due to the fact that frequent communion was no longer common in his time and, in any case, of little interest visually, unlike the splendor of the processions earlier in the liturgy. After communion, the deacons took the vessels back to the skeuophylakion. A deacon exclaimed "Let us depart in peace," and the "Prayer behind the ambo" was read in the nave as the clergy processed out of the church.[33]

Such, in brief was the shape of the liturgy in Germanus' day. The scope of this introduction makes a more complete description impossible, but the reader is encouraged to

---

[32]The anaphora was recited silently in Constantinople since at least the sixth century. Cf the references in Taft, "The Liturgy of the Great Church," 56, footnote 64.

[33]Cf Mathews, *The Early Churches,* 172-173.

pursue the subject by reviewing the works cited in the footnotes.[34]

THE PLACE OF GERMANUS
IN THE TRADITION

As with any theological work, Germanus' commentary can only be appreciated in its proper context. Thus it is important to know the state of the liturgy which he describes. Equally important is an understanding and appreciation for the literary genre into which the commentary fits, as well as for the theological and historical currents out of which it arose. In short, the *Ecclesiastical History* must be viewed within the perspective of tradition to be properly understood. Without such an approach, the work appears highly confusing, at times self-contradictory, at best an allegory.

A. *The Genre of the Liturgical Commentary*

The liturgical commentary has its origins in the fourth century, with the famous mystagogical catecheses of such leading figures as Cyril of Jerusalem, Ambrose of Milan, and John Chrysostom. Their purpose was to explain the Christian mysteries, baptism and eucharist in particular, to the masses of people who began flocking into the church after its transformation from a persecuted minority to the official state religion. Originally in oral form only—delivered as sermons during the octave of Easter—the mystagogical catecheses were soon written down and widely distributed. They remained popular and useful even after the initial,

---

[34]Taft, *The Great Entrance* also has an exhaustive and up-to-date bibliography, xiii-xxii.

massive influx of converts, for they were a valuable teaching tool, particularly when the predominant mode of entrance into the church shifted to infant baptism, and the emphasis shifted from catechesis proper to instruction and formation of young people. The large number of persons who joined the church chiefly for political or social gain also ensured the survival of this type of instructional literature. In short, the goal of the commentary was to make its recipients understand the meaning of what they were supposed to experience in the liturgy, as well as to inspire in them a feeling of awe and fear. This latter element began to be increasingly emphasized in reaction to the large numbers who participated only nominally in church life, and who therefore needed prodding. The commentary was thus a very useful teaching tool.

The mystagogues found a ready method for their commentaries in the long-standing tradition of biblical exegesis. For, already in the New Testament, scripture is seen as having both a literal and a spiritual meaning. For example, we find the following texts in the Gospels: "You search the scriptures, because you think that in them you have eternal life; and it is they that witness to me" (Jn 5:39); "And beginning with Moses and all the prophets, he interpreted to them in all the scriptures the things concerning himself" (Lk 24:27). Everything in the Old Testament is perceived as referring to Christ, as being fulfilled in Him and thus receiving its true meaning in Him. Adam was "a type of the one who was to come" (Rm 5:14). This is the spiritual meaning of the text, and it is not secondary to the literal meaning, but of at least equal importance. By the fourth century, the "spiritual" level had been further subdivided into three levels:

1. The allegorical level—interprets the Old Testament as referring to Christ and the Church. It is the dogmatic level.

2. The tropological level—relates the allegorical sense to our Christian life. It is the moral level.

3. The anagogical level—refers us to the final consummation in the Kingdom and to our present contemplation of this future, heavenly reality. It is the eschatological aspect.[35]

It was thus natural for the composers of the mystagogies to apply this method to the words and actions of the liturgy. They understood the liturgy, like scripture, to be a channel leading to God, a means of experiencing divine life here and now. Whereas the Old Testament is only a foreshadowing of what is to come, in the church, in its liturgy, the final fulfillment is already *present* and can be experienced. The eucharist is *already* the banquet of the Kingdom, baptism is *already* the victory over death and passage into redeemed life. This exegetical method was thus a most appropriate tool to present all these different levels and to keep them in dynamic tension.

Moreover, this method was used by all the patristic authors: but each of them tended to stress one or another level, depending upon his theological presuppositions and goals. In general, the Antiochene writers stressed the more literal and historical aspect, focusing on the history of salvation and the humanity of Christ. Thus they often interpreted the liturgy as representing Christ's earthly ministry. The Alexandrian authors, heirs to Origen's spiritualizing tendencies, stressed the anagogical level, where the mysteries of the liturgy reveal the ultimate mystery that is God.[36] In the following section, we shall briefly examine a few representative authors of each tradition.

[35]This is outlined in Taft, "The Liturgy of the Great Church," 59-61.

[36]Taft, "The Liturgy of the Great Church," 61. Cf also Bornert, *Les commentaires byzantins,* 60ff., as well as R. Bornert, *"Die*

B. *Pseudo-Dionysius: the Alexandrian Tradition*

Pseudo-Dionysius' commentary on the liturgy is contained in *The Ecclesiastical Hierarchy*.[37] This work, written probably at the very end of the fifth century, describes a Syrian liturgy. The author follows a standard procedure for describing the sacraments: first he defines the sacraments, then he describes the rite, and finally he gives its meaning in a section entitled *theoria*. His method is almost exclusively anagogical: "The sensible rites are the image of the intelligible realities. They lead there and show the way to them" (II, 3, 2). Reality, therefore, is spiritual, and the material symbols are only the means by which it is communicated.[38] Thus the material world has value only insofar as it is symbolic, that is, only insofar as it is able to communicate, to reveal the spiritual realities. The symbol thus becomes a means of spiritual ascent: ". . . It is by means of sensible images that we raise ourselves as much as is possible to divine contemplation" (I, 2). This ascent is, for Dionysius, primarily intellectual (III, 3, 12). Thus "the liturgy is an allegory of the soul's progress from the divisiveness of sin to the divine communion, through a process of purification, illumination, perfection, imaged forth in the rites."[39] Dionysius hardly mentions Christ's earthly ministry, His death and resurrection. The only Christological element focuses on the incarnation as the source of our union with God, which is made possible by our participation in the liturgy:

Symbolgestalt der byzantinischen Liturgie," Archiv für Liturgiewissenschaft 12 (1970) *passim.*

[37]Greek text in PG 3, 369-485. An English translation can be found in T. L. Campbell, trans., *Dionysius the Pseudo-Areopagite: The Ecclesiastical Hierarchy* (Lanham, New York, London: University Press of America, 1981).

[38]Bornert, *Les commentaires byzantins,* 67.

[39]Taft, "The Liturgy of the Great Church," 61.

... By bringing Jesus Christ before our eyes, the bishop thus shows in sensible fashion and in image that which is the very life of our soul: he reveals to us how Christ Himself came out of His mysterious, divine sanctuary out of love for man and took on human form, becoming totally incarnate but without any confusion; how Christ descended to our divided condition without any change in His essential unity to and called the human race to association with Himself and His own good gifts, provided that we unite ourselves to His most divine life by imitating it insofar as we can, that we become sufficiently perfect to enter truly into communion with God and the divine mysteries. (III, 3, 13)

Dionysius thus spends very little time on a description of the rite itself:

Let us leave to the imperfect these signs which, as I have said, are magnificently painted in the entrances of the sanctuaries: they will suffice for their contemplation. As for us, in our contemplation of holy communion, let us pass from the effects to the causes. . . . (III, 3, 2)

The entire liturgy is therefore perceived as an ascent from the material to the spiritual, from the multiplicity of lower existence to the unity of the divine. The whole enarxis and Liturgy of the Word are seen as a spiritual preparation, a cleansing, the removal of the impure (catechumens, penitents), as well as of all material thoughts and passions. The focus is exclusively eschatological: there is no place here for Christ's earthly ministry, for His high-priesthood, for His self-oblation.[40] The holiest act of the liturgy is the

---

[40]Taft, "The Liturgy of the Great Church," 62.

fraction, for this is where "the One is symbolically multiplied and divided," thus enabling us "to adhere to it as the members adhere to the entire body, by divine conformity to a life without sin" (III, 3, 12).

The affinities of Pseudo-Dionysius with Origen and with the Alexandrian tradition are obvious. We find the strong spiritualizing trend so characteristic of Origenism. We find the typically Alexandrian focus on the divinity of Christ, with the resulting difficulty in expressing Christ's earthly ministry. The essential salvific act consists of the incarnation alone, which offers us a proper, divine model to imitate. Deification is achieved through ethical imitation of the perfection of the incarnate Logos. The historical Jesus, while not denied, fades into the background. The result of this approach is an imbalanced Christology, an imbalanced soteriology, as well as an imbalanced view of the liturgy, for it pays little attention to what the liturgy itself has to say, to its texts and rites, and imposes its own philosophical presuppositions on them.

C.   *Theodore of Mopsuestia: the Antiochene Tradition*

Whereas Pseudo-Dionysius and the Alexandrians stress the anagogical approach, the Antiochenes emphasize the allegorical, or typological. In scriptural exegesis, the commentators stress the connection of the events and persons in the Old Testament to Christ, Whom they foreshadow. Applied to the liturgy, this method stresses the connection of the rites with the historical Jesus. Thus baptism is understood as the reenactment of the baptism of Jesus in the Jordan, and particularly of His death and resurrection: the eucharist is seen as a memorial not only of the Last Supper, but of the entire earthly ministry of Christ, as well as a prefiguring of the heavenly liturgy. This approach, first seen in the writings of Isidore of Pelusa († ca. 435) and

John Chrysostom, is synthesized by Theodore of Mopsuestia
in his catechetical homilies, written in 392-428.[41]

> The duty of the High Priest of the New Covenant
> is to offer this sacrifice which revealed the nature
> of the New Covenant. We ought to believe that the
> bishop who is now at the altar is playing the part
> of this High Priest, and that the deacons are so to
> speak presenting an image of the liturgy of the in-
> visible powers . . .
>   We must see Christ now as He is led away to
> His passion, and again later when He is stretched
> out on the altar to be immolated for us. This is why
> some of the deacons spread cloths on the altar
> which remind us of winding sheets while others
> stand on either side and fan the air above the
> sacred body . . .[42]

This dual symbolism continues throughout his commentary on the liturgy, contained in Catechetical Homilies
15 and 16. The focus is on Christ's earthly ministry, on
the historical events of His life, which are reenacted and
made present in the rites, as well as on the high priesthood
which Christ now exercises in Heaven.

> It is true that we commemorate our Lord's death
> in food and drink, believing that these are memorials

---

[41]Bornert, *Les commentaires byzantins,* 79-80.

[42]Theodore of Mopsuestia, Homily 15, Synopsis. The best edition, which includes a photographic reproduction of the manuscript
used and a translation into French, is that of R. Tonneau and R.
Devreesse, *Les Homélies Catéchétiques de Théodore de Mopsueste
(Studi e testi* 145) (Vatican: 1949). The text is extremely verbose,
so we take the liberty of quoting from an abbreviated English
translation found in E. Yarnold, *The Awe-Inspiring Rites of Initia-
tion: Baptismal Homilies of the Fourth Century* (Slough: St. Paul
Publications, 1971).

of His passion, since He said himself: "This is my body, which is broken for you." But it is evident also that what we perform in the liturgy is a kind of sacrifice. The duty of the High Priest of the New Covenant is to offer this sacrifice which revealed the nature of the New Covenant. It is clearly a sacrifice, although it is not something that is new or accomplished by the efforts of the bishop: it is a recalling of this true offering. Since the bishop performs in symbols signs of the heavenly realities, the sacrifice must manifest them, so that he presents, as it were, the heavenly liturgy.[43]

We continue in faith until we ascend into heaven and go to our Lord, when we shall no longer see him in a mirror dimly, but face to face. We look forward to attaining to this state of reality at the resurrection, at the time God has ordained; in the meantime we approach the first-fruits of these blessings, Christ our Lord, the High Priest of our inheritance. Accordingly *we are taught to perform in this world the symbols and signs of the blessings to come,* and so, as people who enter into the enjoyment of the good things of heaven by means of the liturgy, we may possess in assured hope what we look for. . . .[44]

Every time, then, there is performed the liturgy of this awesome sacrifice, which is the clear image of the heavenly realities, we should imagine that we are in heaven. Faith enables us to picture in our minds the heavenly realities, as we remind ourselves that the same Christ Who is in heaven, Who died for

---

[43]Homily 15, ch 15.
[44]Homily 15, ch 18.

us, rose again and ascended to heaven, is now immolated under these symbols. So when faith enables
our eyes to contemplate the commemoration that
takes place now, we are brought again to see His
death, resurrection and ascension, which have already taken place for our sake.[45]

In this type of allegorical mystagogy, rites and objects
begin to take on a specific and detailed meaning. The following, for example, is Theodore's description of the Great
Entrance procession, where the gifts are brought to the
altar:

By means of the signs we must see Christ now being
led away to His passion and again later when He is
stretched out on the altar to be immolated for us.
When the offering which is about to be presented
is brought out in the sacred vessels, on the patens
and in the chalice, you must imagine that Christ our
Lord is being led out to His passion. . . .

These signs point to the invisible ministering
powers which were present at the time of the saving
passion and performed their ministry, as they did
throughout our Lord's incarnate life. . . . So you
must regard deacons as representations of the invisible ministering powers when they carry up the
bread for the offering. . . .[46] They bring up the bread
and place it on the altar to complete the representation of the passion. So from now on we should
consider that Christ has already undergone the
passion and is now placed on the altar as if in a
tomb. . . .[47]

---

[45]Homily 15, ch 20.
[46]Homily 15, ch 25.
[47]Homily 15, ch 26.

All this takes place amid general silence; for
since the liturgy has not yet begun, it is appropriate
that everyone should look on in fearful recollection
and silent prayer while this great and august body
is brought and laid out. For when our Lord died,
the disciples also withdrew and remained for a
while in a house in great recollection and fear. . . .[48]

This part of the liturgy is interpreted as representing the
passion and funeral cortege of Christ, and this theme is
continued in the description of the eucharistic prayer, cul-
minating with the epiclesis, or invocation of the Holy Spirit:

. . . This is the moment appointed for Christ our
Lord to rise from the dead and pour out His grace
upon us all. This can take place only by the coming of the grace of the Holy Spirit, by which the
Holy Spirit once raised Christ from the dead. . . .[49]

The same theme is then carried through to the end of the
liturgy:

In the symbols that have been enacted, He rose out
of the dead from the altar, as if from a tomb; He
appears and comes close to us; and when we receive
Him in communion, He announces to us His resurrection.[50]

So the entire liturgy becomes a dramatic reenactment of
the passion of Christ, something which was of little con-
cern to the Alexandrians. Here we see the man Christ
Who, now risen, serves as our High Priest before the throne

[48]Homily 15, ch 28.
[49]Homily 16, ch 11.
[50]Homily 16, ch 26.

of God, but Who is still a man. The ethical element comes
in only in the context of communion:[51]

> You too have been born in baptism by the grace
> and the coming of the Holy Spirit, so that this sancti-
> fication you have been given may strengthen and
> grow, and the promised blessings may be fulfilled
> in the world to come where we shall all enjoy com-
> plete holiness. . . .[52]

We must look to Jerusalem for the development of this
historicizing system of liturgical symbolism, which clearly
depends on an Antiochene exegetical method.[53] In the
fourth century, Jerusalem became a center of pilgrimage,
and Constantine began a massive building campaign to
erect monuments to the new, official religion of the Roman
Empire. Thus churches, basilicas and martyria, were built
on the supposed sites of the chief events of Christ's earthly
ministry. The liturgy which developed here at this time
was a highly stational one—Holy Week, for example, was
comprised of a series of processions to the various holy
sites, with appropriate readings to mark the dramatic events
of Christ's passion. Our best description comes from the
report of the pilgrim Egeria, who visited Jerusalem ca. 381-
384. The following is a description of part of the services
on Holy Friday:

> When the cocks begin to crow, everyone leaves
> the Imbomon,[54] and comes down with singing to the
> place where the Lord prayed, as the Gospels describe

---

[51]Taft, "The Liturgy of the Great Chuch," 65.

[52]Homily 16, ch 23.

[53]Taft, "The Liturgy of the Great Church," 67-68.

[54]A small hill next to the Mount of Olives, where the people
kept vigil on the night from Holy Thursday to Holy Friday.

in the passage which begins, "And he was parted from them about a stone's cast, and prayed" (Lk 22:11). The bishop and all the people go into a graceful church which has been built there, and have a prayer appropriate to the place and the day, and one suitable hymn. . . . From there all of them, including the smallest children, now go down with singing and conduct the bishop to Gethsemane. . . . When everyone arrives at Gethsemane, they have an appropriate prayer, a hymn, and then a reading from the Gospel about the Lord's arrest. By the time it has been read everyone is groaning and lamenting and weeping so loud that the people even across the city can probably hear it all. . . .[55]

It is easy to see how the Antiochene exegetical method took to this historicizing trend.

The structure of the whole church year was strongly influenced by this new approach, but so were individual rites. Baptism, as we can see from the catechetical orations of Cyril of Jerusalem, began to be interpreted chiefly as a reenactment of the death and resurrection of Christ, based on the text of Rm 6:

You . . . submerged yourselves three times in the water and emerged: by this gesture you were secretly re-enacting the burial of Christ's three days in the tomb. For just as our Saviour spent three days and three nights in the hollow bosom of the earth, so you upon first emerging were representing Christ's first day in the earth, and by your immersion his first night. . . . In one and the same action

---

[55]J. Wilkinson, ed., *Egeria's Travels* (London: SPCK, 1971), ch 36, 1-3.

you died and were born: the water of salvation became both tomb and mother for you. . . .[56]

The theme of baptism as sharing in Christ's death and
resurrection is of course not new, but the renewed emphasis on it at this time, and particularly the new mode in
which it is expressed, is the direct result of this new, historicizing trend. From this application to the baptismal
rite, it is but a short step towards such a typology of the
eucharist as well.

From Jerusalem too comes a topographical system of
church symbolism. Thus at daily vespers, called *Lychnicon,*
"All the people congregate once more in the Anastasis,
and the lamps and candles are all lit, which makes it
bright. The fire is brought not from the outside, but from
the cave—inside the screen—where a lamp is always burning night and day. . . ."[57] We are familiar with this rite
from the Byzantine Liturgy of the Pre-sanctified Gifts,
where the priest emerges from the altar with a candle and
exclaims: "The Light of Christ illumines all." The lighting
of the candles at Easter also derives from the same symbolism: the risen Christ, the light of the world, emerges from
the tomb. From here it is but a short step to a whole system
of topological symbolism:

What was spread across the map of Jerusalem's holy
history came to be written small in the humbler
churches of eastern Christendom. . . . Thus the
sanctuary apse becomes the cave of the sepulchre,
and the altar the tomb from which salvation came
forth to the world. . . . Its application to the
eucharist was so congruous as to be inevitable. The

[56]Cyril of Jerusalem, *Catechetical Oration* II, 4. English translation from Yarnold, *Awe-Inspiring Rites,* 76.
[57]*Egeria's Travels,* ch 24, 4.

next step, or perhaps a concomitant one, since the evolutionary sequence is not all that clear, was the burial cortege symbolism at the transfer and deposition of gifts.[58]

D. *Maximus the Confessor*

St Maximus the Confessor (580-662) wrote his *Mystagogy* ca. 630, about a century before Germanus.[59] His is the first properly Byzantine commentary, and is thus of great interest. Addressed to monks, the work is meant to combine the monastic spiritual tradition with the mystagogical.[60] Maximus wanted to show the importance of the liturgy for monastic life, and so to correct a trend which had little use for eucharistic piety. This treatise remains an important source for our knowledge of the Byzantine understanding of the liturgy in the period immediately preceding Germanus.

Maximus approaches the liturgy on two levels, which he calls the "general" (γενικῶς) and the "particular" (ἰδικῶς). For each part of the liturgy, he gives two explanations. The general meaning refers the mystery of salvation to the whole cosmos: this method of interpretation is essentially typological. The particular meaning refers the liturgy to each individual: the process here is anagogical. We can see this from the very beginning of his commentary, when he describes the symbolism of the

---

[58]Taft, "The Liturgy of the Great Church," 66.

[59]Greek text in PG 91, 657-718. An English translation is available in Dom J. Stead, *The Church, the Liturgy and the Soul of Man: the Mystagogia of St Maximus the Confessor* (Still River, MA: St. Bede's Publications, 1982) 57-120.

[60]I.-H. Dalmais, *"Place de la Mystagogie de saint Maxime le Confesseur dans la théologie liturgique byzantine," Studia Patristica* V/3 (= *Texte und Untersuchungen* 80) (Berlin, 1962) 283.

church building. The church is, first, an image of the whole universe:

> The holy church of God . . . is a figure and image of the world, which is composed of visible and invisible things. . . . It is divided into a place reserved for the clergy and assistants, which we call the sanctuary, and a place accessible to all the faithful, which we call the nave. Nevertheless, the church is essentially one, not divided because of the variety of its parts. . . . The wise thus glimpse the universe of things brought into existence by God's creation, divided between the spiritual world, containing incorporeal intelligent substances, and the corporeal world, the object of sense . . . as if they were all another church, not built by hands, but suggested by the ones we build: its sanctuary is the world above, allotted to the powers above, its nave the world below, assigned to those whose lot it is to live in the senses (ch 2).
>
>   . . . the holy church of God is an image of just the sensible world by itself; the sanctuary reminds one of the sky, the dignity of the nave reflects the earth. Likewise the world can be thought of as a church: the sky seems like a sanctuary, and the cultivation of the land can make it resemble a temple (ch 3).

The particular meaning makes the church building symbolic of the individual:

> . . . God's holy church is a symbol of man; its soul is the sanctuary; the sacred altar, the mind; and its body is the nave. A church is thus the image and likeness of man, who was made in the image and likeness of God. The nave is used as the body should

be used, for exemplifying moral philosophy; from the sanctuary the church leads the way to natural contemplation spiritually as man does with his soul; and she embarks in mystical theology through the sacred altar, as man does through his mind (ch 4).

Maximus constantly refers to the *Ecclesistical Hierarchy* of Ps.-Dionysius and is strongly influenced by him. For Maximus, the "general" history of salvation becomes, through the liturgy, a "particular," or mystical history. Each soul expresses the saving plan of God. Thus the eucharistic rites represent the mystical ascension of the soul to contemplation of God, and so to union, with Him.[61] Unlike Ps.-Dionysius, however, Maximus does pay attention to the economy of salvation, for he also sees the liturgy as representing all salvation history, from the incarnation to the final consummation in the world to come. His approach remains essentially Alexandrian, however, in that he pays little attention to the earthly events of the economy of salvation and emphasizes the incarnation of Christ, to the virtual exclusion of the paschal mystery.[62]

Maximus' interpretation of the first entrance of the Byzantine liturgy follows the dual pattern we have seen. He begins with the "general" meaning: "The bishop's first entrance into the holy church at the holy synaxis represents the first coming into the world of the Son of God, Christ our Saviour, in the flesh" (ch 8). In the next chapter, he gives the "particular" meaning: ". . . the people entering the church with the bishop symbolize unbelievers being converted from ignorance and deception to the recognition

---

[61]R. Bornert, *"L'anaphore dans la spiritualité liturgique de Byzance: le témoignage des commentaires mystagogiques du viie au xve siècle," Eucharisties d'Orient et d'Occident* (= *Lex orandi* 47) (Paris, 1970) 245.

[62]Taft, "The Liturgy of the Great Church," 71.

of God, and believers changing over from evil and ignorance to goodness and knowledge . . ." (ch 9). The reading of the Gospel, the descent of the bishop from the throne, the expulsion of the penitents and catechumens symbolize the Second Coming of Christ and the final judgment (chs 14-15). On the "particular" level, these rites represent the "shutting out of the visible world," the "getting rid of thoughts which still incline towards the earth, turning the mind to a vision of spiritual things" (ch 13). Maximus' explanation of the Great Entrance, the anaphora, and communion is straightforward, emphasizing that these are a foretaste of life after the parousia, in the Kingdom.

E. *The Nature of the Liturgical Commentary*

An obvious fact which emerges from even such a brief review of this mystagogical literature is that each commentator, though working from a liturgy which remains essentially unchanged, stresses different elements. This variety stems from the different social and theological conditions in which each commentary was composed. We have already mentioned the influence of the Antiochene and Alexandrian exegetical and theological approaches to scripture, to Christology, to soteriology, as well as the influence of Jerusalem. Without a grasp of the historical and theological context in which they were written, it is clearly difficult properly to understand the liturgical commentaries we have so briefly examined. Indeed, at times it may appear that the commentators have dealt violence to the very essence of the liturgy they were describing: such is the conclusion reached by A. Schmemann, who sees all this literature in a very negative light.[63] What is certainly

[63]*Introduction to Liturgical Theology* (London: Faith Press, 1966) 99-115.

true is that this body of writing marks a shift in piety—
chiefly the decline of frequent communion, beginning already in the fourth century—which created the pastoral
necessity of developing a different rationale for the liturgy.
But there were other, more positive, factors as well.

The decline in frequency of communion was the result
of social factors following the adoption of Christianity as
the state religion after the Peace of Constantine in 313.
There came a massive influx of new members into the
church, and many of them joined more out of political
expediency than out of sincere conversion. In addition,
many apostates, who had left the church during periods
of persecution, now returned. These had to undergo an
extended period of penitence, during which they were
barred from the eucharistic table. Again, numerous persons postponed baptism until a later age, remaining en-
rolled as catechumens for many years—among these are
such figures as the Emperor Constantine, Basil the Great,
and John Chrysostom. The result of all of this was a
fracturing of the community into a communicating minority
and a majority who were in church only as observers. At
first, all the latter were dismissed before the anaphora,
but later they were allowed to remain as onlookers. In the
same century came the development of a spirituality of
fear and awe with regard to the eucharist, and this only
encouraged the flight from the eucharistic banquet—espe-
cially among those whose conversion was only nominal any-
way. Thus a new approach to the liturgy had to arise. The
"Antiochene" response was to develop a symbolism of the
liturgy which saw the presence of the saving works of
Christ in the rites themselves.[64] The "Alexandrian" approach, more spiritualizing, was to develop a kind of
Christian gnoseology, far more mystical and individual-
istic, an approach popular particularly in monastic circles.

---

[64]Taft, "The Liturgy of the Great Church," 68-69.

The theological debates of the period, primarily the conflict with Arianism and the Christological controversies which followed, also had strong impact on the liturgy and on liturgical explanations. The doxological formula ("Glory to the Father, *through* the Son, *in* the Holy Spirit") was levelled in response to the Arian claims that it supported their subordinationism—thus its present form: "Glory to the Father, *and* to the Son, *and* to the Holy Spirit." In the sixth century, the addition to the Byzantine liturgy of the troparion *Ho Monogenes* ("Only-begotten Son") and of the Creed, also came in reaction to current theological disputes. In commentaries on the liturgy, the Antiochene stress on salvation history, particularly on Christ's earthly ministry, was a response to Arianism, as was the Alexandrian stress on Christ's divinity. Maximus, writing to monks who were steeped in Origenistic thought, sought to introduce them to a more historical approach to salvation history, in order to correct their strongly gnostic approach.[65] Because of this, Maximus refers constantly to Ps.-Dionysius, popular among the monks, whose theology Maximus wanted to correct somewhat by adding a greater appreciation for salvation history.

Underlying all these commentaries, therefore, is a sense that the liturgy is itself a source of theology. Just like Scripture, the liturgy is a revelation, which implies a multiplicity of meanings, and indeed offers the possibility for participation in divine life. But the key to a proper understanding of the mystagogies is knowing their historical context. The commentators wrote in response to concrete social and theological issues, and only when the issues are known are the responses understandable. If taken out of

---

[65]See for example the discussion on eucharistic theology in Byzantine history in J. Meyendorff, *Byzantine Theology: Historical Trends and Doctrinal Themes* (New York: Fordham University Press, 1974) 200-211.

this context, the commentaries lose much of their meaning, and can in fact become misleading. With all these factors in mind, then, we can now address ourselves to the rather perplexing commentary of Patriarch Germanus of Constantinople.

F. *Germanus: a New Synthesis*

The Byzantine approach to the liturgy before Germanus was basically Alexandrian, following the interpretation of Ps.-Dionysius and Maximus. The notion of the earthly liturgy as representing the heavenly liturgy predominated: this is clear from texts of the liturgy, particularly in the Introit Prayer, which we discussed above, and in the text of the Cherubic Hymn: "Let us who mystically represent the Cherubim. . . ." The liturgy was perceived as an ascent into the Kingdom and as the image of the individual soul's conversion and ascent to union with God, for which the incarnation served as the model.[66] For Maximus, the liturgy also represented the entire economy of salvation to the parousia and final consummation: thus even in this somewhat more historical approach the emphasis remained primarily eschatological.

Germanus keeps much of this earlier Byzantine tradition, modifying it somewhat, and adds a more Antiochene perspective, far more historicizing and focusing on the human ministry of Christ. This is apparent from the very beginning of his commentary: "The church is an earthly heaven in which the supercelestial God dwells and walks about. It represents the crucifixion, burial, and resurrection of Christ" (ch 1). Immediately we are presented with this

---

[66]Taft, "The Liturgy of the Great Church," 70-71. For a more detailed discussion, see Bornert, *Les commentaires byzantins,* 110-123.

dual approach. As his readers would have been more familiar with the more traditional, eschatological approach, Germanus spends more time on the newer, less familiar, interpretation. Thus "the apse corresponds to the cave in Bethlehem where Christ was born, as well as the cave in which He was buried" (ch 3), the "holy table corresponds to the spot in the tomb where Christ was placed" and the table at which Christ sat with his disciples at the Last Supper (ch 4). The ambo represents the stone at the Holy Sepulchre from which the angel proclaimed Christ's resurrection (ch 10) and from which the deacon, who represents the angel (ch 16), proclaims the Gospel. Thus the building, the vestments, the celebrants, the rites all symbolize and reveal Christ's earthly ministry. But the old symbolism does not disappear:

> The altar is and is called the heavenly and spiritual altar, where the earthly and material priests who always assist and serve the Lord represent the spiritual, serving, and hierarchical powers of the immaterial and celestial powers, for they also must be as a burning fire. For the Son of God and Judge of all ordained the laws and established the services of both the heavenly and the earthly [powers]. (ch 6).

We are back in the Dionysian world here.

The vestments of the clergy are similarly given these two levels of meaning. Predominant is the theme of Christ's earthly ministry, as well as priestly symbolism from the Old Testament. Thus the stole is seen as "the robe of Aaron," its red color pointing to Christ's "undefiled blood on the cross" (ch 14). The embroidery on the vestments signifies the bonds placed on Christ and the blood flowing from his side (ch 17). The interpolations give similar interpretations to articles of the monastic habit. But the theme of

the heavenly liturgy is also present. For the presbyters represent the Cherubim, their stoles like cherubic wings: the deacons are images of the angels, their linen oraria like wings (ch 16).

The prothesis rite is interpreted as representing the sacrifice of Christ, using, once again, Old Testament imagery. We can clearly see in process the development of the present Byzantine rite, for what in ch 21 is presented as a symbolic *interpretation* of the cutting out of the eucharistic lamb becomes, a century later, part of the text of the newly expanded rite.

The antiphons are seen as prophecies of the incarnation. Pss 92 and 94 are quoted ("He is clothed in majesty" and "Come let us worship and fall down before him") in chs 23-24; these, together with Ps 91, were the normal Sunday antiphons at that time.[67] These prophecies are fulfilled at the entrance, which signifies the incarnation, the coming of the Son of God into this world (ch 24). This theme is again continued with the Trisagion which, in addition to being the angelic hymn, represents our gifts to the incarnate Lord, faith, hope, and love, like the gold, frankincense, and myrrh of the Magi. Similarly, the prokeimenon and the alleluia psalm prophesy the coming of Christ (παρουσία), which is fulfilled in the reading of the Gospel. "The Gospel is the coming of God . . . no longer speaking to us as through a cloud . . . but visibly as a true man . . . face to face, and not through riddles" (ch 31). Thus the incarnate Lord is seen as being visibly present in the Liturgy of the Word.[68] Whereas for Maximus the Gospel already symbolized the second coming of Christ, the emphasis here is less

---

[67]See J. Mateos, *La célébration de la parole dans la liturgie byzantine* (= *Orientalia Christiana Analecta* 191) (Rome: 1971) 46-49.

[68]Taft, "The Liturgy of the Great Church," 52.

eschatological, more historical, and the second coming is only anticipated in 6500 years (ch 33).

After discussing the Gospel, the prayer and dismissal of the catechumens, Germanus goes on to the Cherubic Hymn. He begins with the traditional Byzantine explanation:

> By means of the procession of the deacons and the representation of the fans, which are in the likeness of the seraphim, the Cherubic Hymn signifies the entrance of all the saints and righteous ahead of the cherubic powers and the angelic hosts, who run invisibly in advance of the great king, Christ . . . (ch 37).

This is consistent with the meaning of the rite as expressed in the text of the Prayer of the Proskomede and the Cherubic Hymn. This part of the liturgy, then, represents our preparation for the mystery which is about to occur, and is as well a memorial of the earthly economy of salvation:

> . . . The spiritual powers and the choirs of angels, who have seen His spiritual dispensation fulfilled through the cross and death of Christ, the victory over death which has taken place, the descent into hell, and the resurrection on the third day, with us exclaim the alleluia (ch 37).

The Holy Spirit too is present, "seen spiritually in the fire, incense, smoke, and fragrant air" (ch 37). Thus the Great Entrance is a "prolepsis of the entire eucharistic anamnesis" and serves to introduce the rite which follows.[69] Though less eschatologically oriented than Maximus, who

---

[69]Taft, "The Liturgy of the Great Church," 54.

sees the entrance as showing the second coming and final consummation, Germanus nevertheless maintains the traditional Byzantine symbolism of this part of the liturgy.

To this primitive layer, Germanus then adds a different, Antiochene interpretation. The Great Entrance "is also in imitation of the burial of Christ, when Joseph took down the body from the cross, wrapped it in clean linen, anointed it with spices and ointment, carried it with Nicodemus, and placed it in a new tomb hewn out of a rock" (ch 37). Each liturgical vessel and item is then given an allegorical meaning to fit this new conception: the discos represents the hands of Joseph and Nicodemus (ch 38); its cover is the cloth placed over Christ's face in the tomb (ch 40); the aer is the stone sealing the tomb (ch 41) . . . We could be reading Theodore of Mopsuestia here, although Germanus pushes the symbolism much further, to the point that it degenerates into mere allegory. The explanations given for the prothesis rite (chs 20-22), of the eiliton (ch 34), and of the proskomede (ch 36) are nothing more than an extension of this Antiochene symbolism of the Great Entrance to the rites which precede it.

In ch 41, Germanus attempts to fuse the two levels of symbolism:

> Thus Christ is crucified, life is buried, the tomb is secured, the stone is sealed. In the company of the angelic powers, the priest approaches, standing no longer as on earth, but attending at the heavenly altar, before the altar of the throne of God, and he contemplates the great, ineffable, and unsearchable mystery of God.

Then the angel, represented by the deacon, rolls away the stone from the tomb—undoubtedly removing the aer which had been placed over the patens and chalices at the deposition—and proclaims the resurrection: "Let us stand

aright. . . ." The people then proclaim the resurrection: "A mercy of peace, a sacrifice of praise." Then the bishop leads everyone to the heavenly Jerusalem: "Let us lift up our hearts!" And all answer: "We lift them up to the Lord."

The remainder of the commentary is directed to the heavenly mystery, and the funeral cortege symbolism appears no more. The bishop converses directly with God, whom he sees face to face, not through a cloud as did Moses. He is surrounded by angels, represented by the deacons and the ripidia. The people sing the angelic Trisagion, "Holy, holy, holy, Lord of Sabaoth." Germanus says nothing about the text of the anaphora, because this was recited silently by the bishop, "Who is learned in the divine knowledge of the Holy Trinity and faith," and who "alone addresses God" (ch 41).

In the context of his commentary on the anaphora, Germanus inserts his theology of the eucharist. He bases it on the text of Is 6:1-7, which contains the heavenly Trisagion. The bishop holds the spiritual coal in his hands, and this "coal sanctifies those who receive and partake of it." In this, Germanus is following the same use of the text by Theodore of Mopsuestia.[70] Following the angelic Trisagion comes a straightforward explanation of the rest of the anaphora, the memorial of the history of salvation, the consecration by the power of the Holy Spirit. Then come the remembrances of the dead and the living, all of whom "are called together to assemble with the prophets, apostles, and hierarchs in order to recline at the mystical banquet of the Kingdom of Christ with Abraham, Isaac, and Jacob" (ch 44). The commentary concludes with a rather simple presentation of the Lord's Prayer and a brief chapter on communion, based on Hb 9:19ff.

---

[70]Taft, "The Liturgy of the Great Church," 56.

G. *Reasons for this Shift*

The commentary of Germanus marks a clear shift in
the Byzantine perception of the eucharist. This is already
indicated by the title of the work: Ἱστορία ἐκκλησιαστικὴ καὶ μυστικὴ θεωρία—*Ecclesiastical History and
Mystical Contemplation.* In Maximus, and in Ps.-Dionysuis
before him, the focus had been on *theoria,* that is, on the
understanding of the realities which lie *behind* or *over* that
which is visible. Contemplation thus becomes an ascent
from the image to its archetype, and often the image itself
loses its own intrinsic value. Thus the liturgy is seen to be
a means for the contemplation of the Divine Unity, with
little room for the concrete, historical events of the history
of salvation. In contrast to *theoria,* but not opposed to it,
is *historia*: this too is contemplation, but a contemplation
which seeks to clarify the spiritual dimension of an event,
of a rite. Here, the outer forms are taken very seriously
and are not secondary. *Historia* attempts to connect the
words and actions of the liturgy to the history of salvation:
its purpose is to pull the observer into salvation history,
to make the observer a participant in it. Thus *historia*
focuses on the reality of the self-revelation of God in
Christ: *theoria* attempts to lead the graced person to the
reality that is God.[71] Before Germanus, as we have seen,
the anagogical approach predominated in the Byzantine
tradition. Through Germanus, the more historical approach
appears.

The context for this shift is the rise of iconoclasm. The
iconoclasts denied the possibility of any pictorial representation of Christ, and saw the cult of icons as a return to
paganism.[72] Thus the iconoclastic council of 754 declared

[71]See the discussion of these concepts in Bornert, *"Die Symbolgestalt,"* 62ff.

[72]For the history of the development of iconoclasm, see A.

that the eucharist is the only valid symbol of Christ.[73] This same council also condemned Germanus, for Germanus, the first to see that iconoclasm was in fact a rejection of the incarnation, was the first leader of the Orthodox opposition to this movement:

It is not to deviate from the perfect worship of God that we allow the production of icons made of wax and colors. For we make no icon or representation of the invisible divinity: in fact, the holy angels themselves cannot understand or penetrate it totally. But since the only Son himself, Who is in the bosom of the Father, deigned to become man according to the good will of the Father and the Holy Spirit, in order to ransom His own creature from death, since He became a participant in blood and flesh like us, as the great apostle says—"Having become similar to us in everything except sin" (Hb 4:15)—we draw the image of His human aspect according to the flesh, and not according to His incomprehensible and invisible divinity, for we feel the need to represent what is our faith, to show that He is not united to our nature only in appearance, as a shadow . . . but that He has become man in reality and truth, perfect in everything except the sin which the Enemy has sown in us. Because of this unshakable faith in Him, we represent the character of His holy body on the icons, and we venerate and honor them with the reverence due to them,

Grabar, *L'iconoclasme byzantin. Dossier archéologique* (Paris: Collège de France, 1957). For a more detailed study of iconoclasm in Germanus' time, see S. Gero, *Byzantine Iconoclasm during the Reign of Leo III* (= *Corpus Scriptorum Christianorum Orientalium* 346, *Subsidia,* t. 41) (Louvain, 1973).

[73]*Horos* of the council of 754, Mansi 13, 261-264.

because they lead us to the remembrance of His
divine, lifegiving, and inexpressible incarnation.[74]

Further, the Orthodox see the iconoclasts as in fact denying
the two-natures formula of Chalcedon, as well as rejecting
the goodness of the material world: by implication, they
also see the iconoclasts as denying the historical economy
of salvation.

The reaction of the Orthodox was to move to greater
realism. The Council in Trullo, already in 692, declared
that henceforward Christ could only be represented as a
man, and no longer in symbols, such as a lamb.[75] The focus
in iconography thus shifts to a more realistic representation
of Christ, particularly to the details of his earthly life. For
the first time there appear icons representing Christ dead
on the cross, as well as of the resurrected body of Christ.[76]
For what can show Christ's total assumption of our humanity better than his death? And how can we be assured of
our own resurrection if Christ Himself did not rise from
the dead *as a man?*[77]

In its perception of the liturgy, the Antiochene approach
of Theodore of Mopsuestia, with its greater attention to
the historical Jesus and to his humanity, was clearly more
suited to this new, more realistic approach of the Orthodox.
It supported the Orthodox polemic against the iconoclasts
far better than the older, more spiritualizing approach of
the Alexandrians, as formulated in the Byzantine milieu
by Maximus. In fact, the iconoclastic position was heavily

---

[74]Letter to John of Synades, Mansi 13, 101A-C. For a discussion
of the implications of this passage, see C. von Schönborn, *L'icône
du Christ: fondements théologiques* (= *Paradosis* 24) (Fribourg:
Editions Universitaires, 1976) 181-186.

[75]Canon 82, Mansi 11, 977E-980B.

[76]Schönborn, *L'icône du Christ,* 236-237.

[77]For a description of this development in iconographic art, see
Grabar, *L'iconoclasme byzantin,* 228-233.

dependent precisely upon his Origenistic approach, which denigrated the importance of the flesh of Christ—for what they saw as essential was the Logos who dwells in the flesh.[78] It was probably from Ps.-Dionysius that the icono-clasts derived their notion of the eucharist as the only valid "image" and "symbol" of Christ, because only here is the image consubstantial with its prototype,[79] though of course this tradition reaches further back.[80]

In short, the traditional Byzantine approach was no longer fully adequate: more attention had to be paid to the historical man, Jesus. The danger no longer came from the Arians, who had denied Christ's divinity, but from the iconoclasts, who now challenged the dogma of Christ's full humanity, and who in consequence saw the eucharist only as a symbol.

As a result of the iconoclastic controversy, Byzantine "Eucharistic realism," clearly departing from Dion-ysian terminology, was redirected along Christo-logical and soteriological lines; in the Eucharist, man participates in the glorified humanity of Christ, which is not the "essence of God," but a humanity still consubstantial to him and available to him as food and drink.[81]

This shift is clearly reflected in Germanus' commentary. He maintains the traditional, eschatological notion of the heavenly liturgy in his symbolism of the church, and espe-cially in his discussion of the anaphora, which remains very close to the text, except for a brief excursus at the begin-ning of the section. But the Liturgy of the Word takes on

[78]Schönborn, *L'icône du Christ*, 79ff.

[79]See Meyendorff, *Byzantine Theology*, 44.

[80]S. Gero, "The Eucharistic Doctrine of the Byzantine Icono-clasts and Its Sources," *Byzantinische Zeitschrift* 68 (1975) 4-22.

[81]Meyendorff, *Byzantine Theology*, 203.

an allegorical sense, based on the historical economy of
Christ. Yet, for the most part, Germanus does not push
this allegory too far, as happens in such later works as the
Protheoria (11th c.), where the liturgy is reduced to a
dramatic representation of the life, death and resurrection
of Christ, where these symbols lose all connection to the
sacrament, and where each rite takes on a meaning totally
unrelated to its function in the liturgy.[82] In contrast to
this later development, Germanus preserves the proper
reality of the celebration: the liturgy is the memorial of
Christ's sacrifice, the accomplishment of the sacrifices of the
old Law, the anticipation of the celestial liturgy. The focus
remains on the central action of the liturgy, on the Holy
Spirit who, through the epiclesis, consecrates the bread
and the wine.[83]

H. *The Legacy of Germanus*

"The proof of the success of Germanus' synthesis is
its viability: for over six hundred years it reigned with
undisputed primacy over the field of Byzantine liturgical
explanation."[84] Its first worthy challenger was the commentary by Cabasilas in the fourteenth century. The sheer
number of manuscripts which remain—at least fifty between
the 10-15th centuries[85]—is evidence of its popularity. Germanus' recognition at II Nicea (787) as the first defender
of Orthodoxy against the iconoclasm of the emperor, Leo
III, lent even greater authority to his work.

In the realm of the liturgy proper, the *Historia* of
Germanus influenced the development of the rites sur-
rounding the Great Entrance and of the prothesis, which

---

[82]Bornert, *Les commentaires byzantins,* 204.

[83]Bornert, *Les commentaires byzantins,* 171ff.

[84]Taft, "The Liturgy of the Great Church," 74.

[85]Bornert, *"L'anaphore dans la spiritualité liturgique,"* 249.

then existed only in embryonic form. The reader will easily recognize this influence in the text of the present Byzantine liturgy. As we can already see from the interpolation in ch 22, which existed by the time of Anastasius only a century later, the prothesis rite had already acquired its strongly sacrificial tone and absorbed some of the formulae and scriptural phrases used by Germanus in his description of the more primitive rite. We can also recognize traces of Germanus' commentary in the prayers which, in the present-day liturgy, accompany the vesting of the clergy.[86]

A less fortunate legacy, for which Germanus is of course not responsible himself, is the subsequent extension of the "life of Christ" symbolism to every rite of the liturgy, as happens in the above-mentioned *Protheoria* by Nicholas of Andyda.[87] In this work, the ceremonies of the liturgy represent not only the passion, death, and resurrection of Christ, but also all the actions of his public and hidden life. The historical symbolism is guided not by any organic vision of the history of salvation, but by the didactic illustration of a thesis: thus the prothesis represents the virginal conception and hidden life of Jesus in Nazareth; the first entrance is the manifestation of Christ at Jordan; the epistle is the election of the twelve apostles—and so on to the conclusion of the liturgy.[88] These interpretations have no connection whatever either to the texts or the central action of the liturgy, which in fact they only conceal.

In conclusion, we hope that we have shown that Germanus' work, as indeed any theological work, can be understood only in its proper context, both historical and theological. As a product of its time, the commentary

---

[86]See Bornert, *Les commentaires byzantins,* 161-170, for changes in the liturgy reflected in and brought about by Germanus' commentary.

[87]PG 140, 417-468.

[88]Bornert, *Les commentaires byzantins,* 202-204.

represents a significant achievement, for it restored to the text of the anaphora much of its importance. If we remember that this prayer was recited silently since at least the sixth century, and that both Ps.-Dionysius and Maximus virtually ignored it, then Germanus accomplished much in restoring it to its prominent position. To the modern reader, the absence of any emphasis on the reception of communion, the central focus on the Great Entrance and its interpretation in terms of the Antiochene burial-motif, can only be seen as serious deficiencies: indeed, they have properly been criticized.[89] But this hardly detracts from the value of the work, as both a historical and theological document. In this context, at a pivotal period in the church's history, the treatise is indeed remarkable for its theological balance.

---

[89]See, for example, Meyendorff, *Byzantine Theology*, 201ff; as well as Schmemann, *Introduction to Liturgical Theology*, 99ff.

ΙΣΤΟΡΙΑ ΕΚΚΛΗΣΙΑΣΤΙΚΗ
ΚΑΙ
ΜΥΣΤΙΚΗ ΘΕΩΡΙΑ

ΓΕΡΜΑΝΟΥ
᾿Αρχιεπισκόπου Κωνσταντινουπόλεως

ECCLESIASTICAL HISTORY
AND
MYSTICAL CONTEMPLATION

BY GERMANUS
Archbishop of Constantinople

ΙΣΤΟΡΙΑ ΕΚΚΛΗΣΙΑΣΤΙΚΗ ΚΑΙ ΜΥΣΤΙΚΗ ΘΕΩΡΙΑ

ΓΕΡΜΑΝΟΥ
Ἀρχιεπισκόπου Κωνσταντινουπόλεως

1. Ἐκκλησία ἐστὶ ναὸς Θεοῦ, τέμενος ἅγιον, οἶκος προσευχῆς, συνάθροισις λαοῦ, σῶμα Χριστοῦ· ὄνομα αὐτῆς νύμφη Χριστοῦ· τῷ ὕδατι τοῦ βαπτίσματος αὐτοῦ καθαρθεῖσα, καὶ τῷ αἵματι ῥαντισθεῖσα τῷ αὐτοῦ καὶ νυμφικῶς ἐστολισμένη, καὶ τῷ τοῦ ἁγίου Πνεύματος μύρῳ σφραγιζομένη κατὰ τὸν προφητικὸν λόγον· «μύρον ἐκκενωθὲν ὄνομά σοι» καὶ «εἰς ὀσμὴν μύρου σου δραμοῦμεν», ὅτι «ὡς μύρον ἐπὶ κεφαλῆς τὸ καταβαῖνον ἐπὶ πώγωνα, τὸν Ἀαρών».

Ἐκκλησία ἐστὶν ἐπίγειος οὐρανός, ἐν ᾧ* ὁ ἐπουράνιος Θεὸς ἐνοικεῖ καὶ ἐμπεριπατεῖ, ἀντιτυποῦσα τὴν σταύρωσιν καὶ τὴν ταφὴν καὶ τὴν ἀνάστασιν Χριστοῦ· δεδοξασμένη ὑπὲρ τὴν σκηνὴν τοῦ μαρτυρίου Μωσέως, ἐν ᾗ τὸ ἱλαστήριον καὶ τὰ Ἅγια τῶν Ἁγίων· ἐν πατριάρχαις προτυπωθεῖσα, ἐν προφήταις προκηρυχθεῖσα, ἐν ἀποστόλοις θεμελιωθεῖσα, ἱεράρχαις κατακοσμηθεῖσα καὶ ἐν μάρτυσι τελειωθεῖσα.

2. Τὸ σήμαντρον αἰνίττεται τὰς τῶν Ἀγγέλων σάλπιγ-

---

*Because of printing difficulties it was not possible to include the iota subscript with certain words, chiefly personal pronouns, which begin with vowels. We apologize to our readers.

ECCLESIASTICAL HISTORY
AND
MYSTICAL CONTEMPLATION

BY GERMANUS
Archbishop of Constantinople

1. The church is the temple of God, a holy place, a house of prayer, the assembly of the people, the body of Christ. It is called the bride of Christ. It is cleansed by the water of His baptism, sprinkled by His blood, clothed in bridal garments, and sealed with the ointment of the Holy Spirit, according to the prophetic saying: "Your name is oil poured out" (Cant 1:3), and "We run after the fragrance of your myrrh" (Cant 1:4), which is[1] "Like the precious oil, running down upon the beard, the beard of Aaron" (Ps 132:2 LXX).

The church is an earthly heaven in which the super-celestial God dwells and walks about. It represents the crucifixion, burial, and resurrection of Christ: it is glorified more than the tabernacle of the witness of Moses, in which are the mercy-seat and the Holy of Holies. It is prefigured in the patriarchs, foretold by the prophets, founded in the apostles, adorned by the hierarchs, and fulfilled in the martyrs.

2. The simandron[2] represents the trumpets of the

---

[1] The Greek text here is read as ὅ τι rather than ὅτι.

[2] σήμαντρον—a long, wooden sounding-board, which is struck to call the faithful to prayer. It is still used in many Greek monasteries.

γας· διεγείρει δὲ καὶ τοὺς ἀγωνιστὰς πρὸς τὸν τῶν ἀοράτων ἐχθρῶν πόλεμον.

3. Κόγχη ἐστὶ κατὰ τὸ ἐν Βηθλεὲμ σπήλαιον, ὅπου ἐγεννήθη ὁ Χριστός· καὶ κατὰ τὸ σπήλαιον ὅπου ἐτάφη, καθὼς φησιν ὁ εὐαγγελιστὴς Μᾶρκος ὅτι «ἦν σπήλαιον λελατομημένον ἐκ πέτρας, ἐκεῖ καὶ ἔθηκαν τὸν Ἰησοῦν»

4. Ἡ ἁγία τράπεζά ἐστιν ἀντὶ τοῦ τόπου ἔνθα ἐτέθη ἐν τῇ ταφῇ ὁ Χριστός· ἐν ᾗ πρόκειται ὁ ἀληθινὸς καὶ οὐράνιος Ἄρτος, ἡ μυστικὴ καὶ ἀναίμακτος θυσία, ζωοθυτούμενος τὴν σάρκα αὐτοῦ καὶ τὸ αἷμα εἰς βρῶσιν ζωῆς αἰωνίου, προέθηκε τοῖς πιστοῖς.

Ἔστι δὲ καὶ θρόνος Θεοῦ ἐν ᾧ ὁ ἐπὶ τῶν χερουβὶμ ἐποχούμενος Θεὸς σωματωθεὶς ἀνεπαύσατο· καθ᾿ ἣν τράπεζαν καὶ ἐν τῷ μυστικῷ αὐτοῦ δείπνῳ, μέσον τῶν αὐτοῦ μαθητῶν καθίσας, καὶ λαβὼν ἄρτον καὶ οἶνον εἶπε τοῖς αὐτοῦ μαθηταῖς καὶ ἀποστόλοις· «λάβετε φάγετε, καὶ πίετε ἐξ αὐτοῦ· τοῦτό ἐστι τὸ σῶμά μου καὶ τὸ αἷμά μου». Προετυπώθη δὲ καὶ ἐν τῇ νομικῇ τραπέζῃ ἔνθα ἦν τὸ μάννα, ὅ ἐστι ὁ Χριστός, ἐξ οὐρανοῦ καταβάς.

5. Τὸ κιβώριόν ἐστι ἀντὶ τοῦ τόπου ἔνθα ἐσταυρώθη ὁ Χριστός· ἐγγὺς γὰρ ἦν ὁ τόπος καὶ ὑπόβαθρος ἔνθα ἐτάφη· ἀλλὰ διὰ τὸ ἐν συντομίᾳ ἐκφέρεσθαι τὴν σταύρωσιν, τὴν ταφὴν καὶ τὴν ἀνάστασιν τοῦ Χριστοῦ ἐν τῇ Ἐκκλησίᾳ τέτακται.

Ἔστι δὲ καὶ κατὰ τὴν κιβωτὸν τῆς διαθήκης Κυρίου, ἐν ᾗ λέγεται Ἅγια Ἁγίων καὶ ἁγίασμα αὐτοῦ· ἐν ᾗ προσέταξεν ὁ Θεὸς γενέσθαι δύο χερουβὶμ ἑκατέρωθεν τορευτά· τὸ γὰρ ΚΙΒ ἐστι κιβωτός, τὸ δὲ ΟΥΡΙΝ φωτισμὸς Θεοῦ, ἢ φῶς Θεοῦ.

angels and calls the contestants to battle against the invisible
enemies.

3. The apse corresponds to the cave in Bethlehem
where Christ was born, as well as the cave in which he
was buried, as the evangelist Mark says: "There was a
cave hewn out of rock; there they placed Jesus" (cf Mk
15:46).[3]

4. The holy table corresponds to the spot in the tomb
where Christ was placed. On it lies the true and heavenly
bread, the mystical and unbloody sacrifice. Christ sacrifices
His flesh and blood and offers it to the faithful as food for
eternal life.

The holy table is also the throne of God, on which,
borne by the Cherubim, He rested in the body. At that
table, at His mystical supper, Christ sat among His disciples and, taking bread and wine, said to His disciples
and apostles: "Take, eat, and drink of it: this is my body
and my blood" (cf Mt 26:26-28). This table was prefigured by the table of the Old Law upon which the manna,
which was Christ, descended from heaven.

5. The ciborium[4] represents here the place where
Christ was crucified; for the place where He was buried was
nearby and raised on a base. It is placed in the church in
order to represent concisely the crucifixion, burial, and
resurrection of Christ.

It similarly corresponds to the ark of the covenant of
the Lord in which, it is written, is His Holy of Holies and
His holy place. Next to it God commanded that two
wrought Cherubim be placed on either side (cf Ex 25:18)
—for *KIB* is the ark, and *OURIN* is the effulgence, or the
light, of God.

---

[3]The phrasing of the Greek text is in fact closer to Jn 19:41-42.
[4]κιβώριον—a large canopy over the altar table, consisting of
four columns and a roof. At Hagia Sophia, it was made of silver.

6. Θυσιαστήριόν ἐστι κατὰ τὸ ἅγιον μνῆμα τοῦ Χριστοῦ· ἐν ᾧ θυσίαν ἑαυτὸν προσήγαγε τῷ Θεῷ καὶ Πατρὶ διὰ τῆς προσφορᾶς τοῦ σώματος αὐτοῦ, ὡς ἀμνὸς θυόμενος, καὶ ὡς ἀρχιερεὺς καὶ υἱὸς ἀνθρώπου προσφέρων καὶ προσφερόμενος εἰς μυστικὴν καὶ ἀναίμακτον θυσίαν καὶ λογικὴν λατρείαν τοῖς πιστοῖς ἱεροθυτούμενος, δι᾽ ἧς μέτοχοι γεγόναμεν ζωῆς αἰωνίου καὶ ἀθανάτου. Ὅνπερ ἀμνὸν προετύπωσεν ἐν Αἰγύπτῳ Μωσῆς πρὸς ἑσπέραν, καὶ τῷ αἵματι αὐτοῦ τὸν ὀλοθρευτὴν ἀπέστρεψε, τοῦ μὴ θανατῶσαι τὸν λαόν. Τὸ γὰρ πρὸς ἑσπέραν σημαίνει ὅτι πρὸς ἑσπέραν ἐσφαγιάσθη ὁ ἀληθινὸς ἀμνὸς καὶ τοῦ κόσμου αἴρων τὴν ἁμαρτίαν ἐν τῷ σταυρῷ αὐτοῦ· καὶ γὰρ τὸ «Πάσχα ἡμῶν ὑπὲρ ἡμῶν ἐτύθη Χριστός».

Θυσιαστήριόν ἐστι καὶ λέγεται κατὰ τὸ ἐπουράνιον καὶ νοερὸν θυσιαστήριον ἐν ᾧπερ ἀντιτυποῦσι τὰς νοερὰς καὶ λειτουργικὰς καὶ ἱεραρχικὰς δυνάμεις τῶν ἀΰλων καὶ ἄνω δυνάμεων· καὶ οἱ ἐπίγειοι καὶ ἔνυλοι ἱερεῖς παρεστῶτες καὶ λατρεύοντες τῷ Κυρίῳ διαπαντός, ὥστε καὶ τοιούτους δεῖ εἶναι ὡς πῦρ φλέγον. Καὶ γὰρ τὴν τῶν ἐπουρανίων ἀκολουθίαν καὶ τὴν τῶν ἐπιγείων διέταξεν ὁ Υἱὸς τοῦ Θεοῦ καὶ κριτὴς τῶν ἁπάντων ἐνομοθέτησε.

7. Βῆμά ἐστιν ὑπόβαθρος τόπος καὶ θρόνος ἐν ᾧπερ ὁ παμβασιλεὺς Χριστὸς προκάθηται μετὰ τῶν αὐτοῦ ἀποστόλων, ὡς πρὸς αὐτοὺς λέγει ὅτι «καθίσεσθε ἐπὶ θρόνων κρίνοντες τὰς δώδεκα φυλὰς τοῦ Ἰσραήλ»· ὑποδεικνύων δὲ τὴν δευτέραν παρουσίαν καθ᾽ ἣν ἔλθῃ καθιὼν ἐπὶ θρόνου ἐνδόξου εἰς τὸ κρῖναι τὸν κόσμον, ὡς λέγει ὁ προφήτης ὅτι «ἐκάθισαν θρόνοι εἰς κρίσιν ἐπὶ οἶκον Δαβίδ».

6. The altar corresponds to the holy tomb of Christ. On it Christ brought Himself as a sacrifice to [His] God and Father through the offering of His body as a sacrificial lamb, and as highpriest and Son of Man, offering and being offered as a mystical bloodless sacrifice, and appointing for the faithful reasonable worship, through which we have become sharers in eternal and immortal life. This lamb Moses prefigured in Egypt "towards evening" when its blood turned back the destroyer so that he would not kill the people (cf Ex 12:7-13). The expression "towards evening" signifies that towards evening the true lamb is sacrificed, the One who takes away the sin of the world on his cross, "For Christ, our Pascha, has been sacrificed for us" (cf I Cor 5:7).

The altar is and is called the heavenly and spiritual altar, where the earthly and material priests who always assist and serve the Lord represent the spiritual, serving, and hierarchical powers of the immaterial and celestial Powers, for they also must be as a burning fire. For the Son of God and Judge of all ordained the laws and established the services of both the heavenly and the earthly (powers).[5]

7. The bema[6] is a concave place, a throne on which Christ, the king of all, presides with His apostles, as He says to them: "You shall sit on thrones judging the twelve tribes of Israel" (Mt 19:28). It points to the second coming, when He will come sitting on the throne of glory to judge the world, as the prophet says: "Thrones were set for judgment over the house of David" (Ps 121:5).

---

[5]Here, the variant reading of Brightman—διάταξιν—is preferred to διέταξεν.

[6]βῆμα—the term refers generally to the whole sanctuary area, and specifically to the elevated area containing the throne. Cf Lampe, *Patristic Greek Lexicon* (Oxford: Clarendon Press, 1961) 295-6.

8. Κοσμήτης ἐστὶ κατὰ τὸ νομικὸν καὶ ἅγιον κόσμιον ἐμφαίνων τὸ τοῦ σταυρωθέντος Χριστοῦ τοῦ Θεοῦ ἐκσφράγισμα διὰ σταυροῦ κοσμούμενον.

9. Κάγκελλά εἰσι τὸν τῆς προσευχῆς τόπον δηλοῦντα, ἐν ᾧ σημαίνει τὴν μὲν ἔξωθεν τοῦ λαοῦ εἴσοδον· τὴν δὲ ἔσωθεν τὰ ῞Αγια τῶν ῾Αγίων ὑπάρχουσαν καὶ μόνοις τοῖς ἱεροῖς οὖσαν ἐπίβατον. ῎Εστι δὲ ὡς ἀληθῶς εἰς ἅγιον μνῆμα κάγκελλα χαλκᾶ διὰ τὸ μηδένα εἰσιέναι ἐν αὐτῷ ἁπλῶς ὡς ἔτυχε.

10. ῾Ο ἄμβων ἐστὶν ἐμφαίνων τὸ σχῆμα τοῦ λίθου τοῦ ἁγίου μνήματος [ὃν ὁ ἄγγελος ἀποκυλίσας ἐκ τῆς θύρας ἐκάθητο ἐπάνω αὐτοῦ πλησίον τῆς θύρας τοῦ μνήματος] ἀναβοῶν τὴν ἀνάστασιν τοῦ Κυρίου ταῖς μυροφόροις. ῎Εστι δὲ καὶ κατὰ τὸν προφήτην τὸν λέγοντα· [«ἐπ᾽ ὄρους πεδινοῦ ἄρατε σημεῖον»], ἀνάβηθι ὁ εὐαγγελιζόμενος καὶ «ὕψωσον φωνήν»· ὄρος γάρ ἐστιν (ὁ ἄμβων) εἰς τόπον πεδινὸν καὶ ὁμαλὸν κείμενος.

11. Τὸ κατὰ ἀνατολὰς εὔχεσθαι παραδεδομένον ἐστίν, ὡς καὶ τὰ λοιπὰ τῶν ἁγίων ἀποστόλων· ἐστὶν οὕτως διὰ τὸν ἥλιον τὸν νοητὸν τῆς δικαιοσύνης Χριστὸν τὸν Θεὸν ἡμῶν ἐπὶ γῆς φανῆναι ἐπὶ τοῖς μέρεσι τῆς ἀνατολῆς τοῦ αἰσθητοῦ ἡλίου, κατὰ τὸν προφήτην τὸν λέγοντα· «ἀνατολὴ ὄνομα αὐτῷ», καὶ πάλιν· «προσκυνήσατε τῷ Κυρίῳ πᾶσα ἡ γῆ, τῷ ἐπιβεβηκότι ἐπὶ τὸν οὐρανὸν τοῦ οὐρανοῦ κατὰ ἀνατολάς», καί· «προσκυνήσωμεν εἰς τόπον οὗ ἔστησαν οἱ πόδες αὐτοῦ», καὶ πάλιν· «στήσονται οἱ πόδες τοῦ Κυρίου ἐπὶ τὸ ὄρος τῶν ἐλαιῶν κατὰ ἀνατολήν». Ταῦτα φασὶν οἱ προφῆται, καὶ διὰ τὸ παραδοκεῖν ἡμᾶς πάλιν τὸν ἐν ἐδὲμ παράδεισον τὸν κατὰ

8. The entablature[7] is the legal and holy decoration, representing a depiction of the crucified Christ by means of a decorated cross.

9. The chancel barriers indicate the place of prayer: the outside is for the people, and the inside, the Holy of Holies, is accessible only to the priests. The barriers, made of bronze, are like those around the Holy Sepulchre,[8] so that no one might enter there by accident.

10. The ambo[9] manifests the shape of the stone at the Holy Sepulchre [on which the angel sat after he rolled it away from the doors of the tomb,] proclaiming the resurrection of the Lord to the myrrhbearing women (cf Mt 28:2-7). This is according to the words of the prophet, ["On a bare hill raise a signal" (Is 13:2)] "Climb, O herald of good tidings, lift up your voice with strength" (Is 40:9). For the ambo is a mountain situated in a flat and level place.

11. Praying toward the East is handed down by the holy apostles, as is everything else. This is because the comprehensible sun of righteousness, Christ our God, appeared on earth in those regions of the East where the perceptible sun rises, as the prophet says: "Orient is his name" (Zech 6:12); and "Bow before the Lord, all the earth, who ascended to the heaven of heavens in the East" (cf Ps 67:34); and "Let us prostrate ourselves in the place where His feet stood" (cf Ps 67:34); and again, "The feet of the Lord shall stand upon the Mount of Olives in the East" (Zech 14:4). The prophets also speak

---

[7]κοσμήτης—the entablature is the decoration on the chancel barriers.

[8]In Jerusalem, built by Constantine.

[9]ἄμβων—a large, oval platform, supported by eight columns, located near the center of the nave. Litanies and readings were proclaimed from it.

ἀνατολὴν ἀπολαμβάνειν· καὶ ὡς οὖν ἐσχομένους τὴν ἀνατολὴν τῆς φωτοφανείας τῆς δευτέρας τοῦ Χριστοῦ καὶ τοῦ Θεοῦ ἡμῶν παρουσίας.

12. Τὸ μὴ κλίνειν τὸ γόνυ ἐν τῇ ἀναστασίμῳ ἡμέρα σημαίνει τὴν τῆς καταπτώσεως ἡμῶν ἀνόρθωσιν τὴν γενομένην διὰ τῆς τριημέρου τοῦ Χριστοῦ ἀναστάσεως.

13. Τὸ δὲ μέχρι τῆς πεντηκοστῆς μὴ κλίνειν τὸ γόνυ ἐστὶ τὰς ἑπτὰ ἡμέρας μετὰ τὸ ἅγιον πάσχα ἑπταπλατουμένας κρατεῖν· τὸ ἑπτάσιν ἑπτὰ τεσσαράκοντα ἐννέα, καὶ ἡ κυριακὴ πεντήκοντα.

Ὁ ἐν τῇ κεφαλῇ τοῦ ἱερέως διπλοῦς στέφανος ἐκ τῆς τῶν τριχῶν σημειώσεως εἰκονίζει τὴν τοῦ κορυφαίου ἀποστόλου Πέτρου κάραν τιμίαν, ἧνπερ ἐν τῷ τοῦ Κυρίου διδασκαλικῷ κηρύγματι ἀποσταλεὶς καὶ ἀποκαρθεὶς ὑπὸ τῶν ἀπειθούντων τῷ λόγῳ, ὡς ἐμπαιζόμενος ὑπ' αὐτῶν. Ταύτην ὁ διδάσκαλος Χριστὸς εὐλόγησε καὶ ἐποίησε τὴν ἀτιμίαν τιμήν, καὶ τὴν χλεύην εἰς δόξαν, καὶ «ἔθηκεν ἐπὶ τὴν κεφαλὴν αὐτοῦ στέφανον οὐκ ἐκ λίθων τιμίων», ἀλλὰ τῷ λίθῳ καὶ τῇ πέτρα τῆς πίστεως αὐτοῦ ἐκλάμπουσαν ὑπὲρ χρυσίον καὶ τοπάζιον καὶ λίθους τιμίους. Κορυφὴ γὰρ καὶ καλλόπισμα καὶ στέφανος τοῦ δωδεκαλίθου, οἵτινές εἰσιν ἀπόστολοι, Πέτρος ὁ παναγιώτατος ὑπάρχει ἱεράρχης Χριστοῦ.

14. Ἡ στολὴ τοῦ ἱερέως ὑπάρχει κατὰ τὸν ποδήριν Ἀαρὼν τὸ μέχρι τῶν ποδῶν ἔνδυμα διῆκον· ὅτι δέ ἐστι πυροειδὴς κατὰ τὸν προφήτην τὸν λέγοντα· «ὁ ποιῶν τοὺς ἀγγέλους αὐτοῦ πνεύματα καὶ τοὺς λειτουργοὺς αὐτοῦ πυρὸς φλόγα» καὶ πάλιν· «τίς οὕτως ὁ παραγενόμενος ἐξ Ἐδώμ»; Ἐδώμ δὲ ἑρμηνεύεται, γήινος, ἐκλεκτός, κόκκινος· εἶτα ἐπάγει· «ἐρύθημα ἱματίων αὐτοῦ ἐκ Βοσώρ· διὰ τί σου ἐρυθρὰ τὰ ἱμάτια καὶ τὰ ἐνδύματά σου ὡς ἀπὸ πατητοῦ ληνοῦ;» ἐμ-

thus because of our fervent hope of receiving again the paradise in Eden, as well as the dawn of the brightness of the second coming of Christ our God, from the East.

12. We do not kneel on Sunday as a sign that our fall has been corrected through the resurrection of Christ on the third day.

13. We do not kneel until Pentecost because we observe the seven days after Easter seven-fold; seven times seven is forty-nine, and Sunday makes fifty.

The double crown inscribed on the head of the priest through tonsure represents the precious head of the chief-apostle Peter. When he was sent out in the teaching and preaching of the Lord, his head was shaved by those who did not believe his word, as if in mockery. The Teacher Christ blessed this head, changed dishonor into honor, ridicule into praise. He placed on it a crown made not of precious stones, but one which shines more than gold, topaz, or precious stone—with the stone and rock of faith. Peter, the most-holy, the summit, beauty, and crown of the twelve stones, which are the apostles, is the hierarch of Christ.

14. The priestly stole is the robe of Aaron, which served to cover him down to his feet. It was fiery in appearance, as the prophet says: "Who makes the winds your messengers and flames of fire your servants" (Ps 103:4); and again, "Who is this coming from Edom"—for Edom means earthly, chosen, and crimson—and then the prophet adds: "In crimsoned garments from Bozrah?" (Is 63:1a). "Why is your clothing all red, like the garments of one who treads grapes in the vat?" (Is 63:2). By this the

φαίνει δὲ τὴν βαφεῖσαν τοῦ Χριστοῦ στολὴν τῆς σαρκὸς αἵματι τῷ ἀχράντῳ ἐν τῷ σταυρῷ αὐτοῦ. Ὅτι δὲ πάλιν· κοκ-
κίνην χλαμύδα ἐφόρεσεν ἐν τῷ πάθει αὐτοῦ ὁ Χριστός, ἐμφαίνει τοὺς ἀρχιερεῖς ποίου ἀρχιερέως εἰσὶν ὑπασπισταί.

15. Τὸ δὲ ἀπεζωσμένους τοὺς ἱερεῖς περιπατεῖν ἐν
φελωνίοις, δείκνυσι ὅτι καὶ ὁ Χριστὸς ἐν τῷ σταυρῷ ἀπερχόμενος οὕτως ἦν βαστάζων τὸν σταυρὸν αὐτοῦ.

16. Ἐν ταῖς ἄνω λαμπρότησι τῶν οὐρανίων λειτουργῶν
καὶ ἱεραρχιῶν, εἰσὶ πρεσβύτεροι εἰκοσιτέσσαρες καὶ διάκονοι
ἑπτά· οἱ πρεσβύτεροι κατὰ μίμησιν τῶν σεραφικῶν δυνάμεών
εἰσιν ταῖς μὲν στολαῖς δίκην πτερύγων κατακεκαλυμμένοι·
ταῖς δὲ δυσὶν εἶτ' οὖν πτέρυξι τῶν χειλέων τὸν ὕμνον βο-
ῶντες καὶ κατέχοντες τὸν θεῖον καὶ νοητὸν ἄνθρακα Χριστόν, ἐν τῷ θυσιαστηρίῳ λαβίδι τῆς χειρὸς φέροντες· οἱ δὲ
διάκονοι εἰς τύπον τῶν ἀγγελικῶν δυνάμεων ταῖς λεπταῖς τῶν
λινῶν ὠραρίων πτέρυξιν ὡς λειτουργικὰ πνεύματα, εἰς δια-
κονίαν ἀποστελλόμενα περιττῶς ἔχουσιν.

17. Τὰ λωρία τοῦ στιχαρίου εἰσὶ τὰ [ἐν τῇ χειρὶ ἐμφαίνοντα δεσμὰ τοῦ Χριστοῦ· δείσαντες γὰρ αὐτόν φησιν,
ἀπήγαγον πρὸς Καϊάφαν τὸν ἀρχιερέα καὶ τὸν Πιλᾶτον. Τὰ
δὲ] εἰς τὰ πλάγια [τοῦ στιχαρίου λωρία εἰσὶ] κατὰ τὸ αἷμα
τὸ ῥεῦσαν ἐκ τῆς πλευρᾶς τοῦ Χριστοῦ.

18. Τὸ Ἐπιτραχήλιόν ἐστι τὸ φακιόλιον μεθ' οὗ ἐπε-
φέρετο ὑπὸ τοῦ ἀρχιερέως δεδεμένος καὶ συρόμενος ἐπὶ τὸ
πρόσθεν ἐκ τοῦ τραχήλου ὁ Χριστὸς ἐν τῷ πάθει αὐτοῦ
ἀπερχόμενος.

19. Τὸ Ὠμοφόριόν ἐστι κατὰ τὴν στολὴν τοῦ Ἀαρών,
ὅπερ ἐφόρουν καὶ οἱ ἐν νόμῳ ἀρχιερεῖς σουδαρίοις μακροῖς,
τὸ δ' εὐώνυμον ὦμον περιτιθέντες. [Τὸ τοῦ ἐπισκόπου ὠμοφόριον ἐξ ἐρίου ὂν καὶ οὐ λινοῦ, τὴν τοῦ προβάτου δορὰν σημαίνει ὅπερ πλανηθὲν ὁ Κύριος εὑρὼν ἐπὶ τὸν ἴδιον ὦμον
ἀνέλαβεν].

prophet indicates the stole of the flesh of Christ dyed by His undefiled blood on the cross. Or, again, since Christ wore a crimson cloak at His passion, it indicates that the high priests are servants of such a High Priest.

15. The fact that priests walk about in unbelted phelonia points out that even Christ thus went to the crucifixion carrying His cross.

16. In the celestial brightness of the heavenly ministers and priests, there are twenty-four presbyters and seven deacons. The presbyters resemble the seraphic powers, covered, as if by wings, with stoles. With two wings, that is, their lips, they proclaim hymns; and they hold the divine and spiritual burning coal, Christ, on the altar with the tongs of their hands. The deacons, images of the angelic powers, go around with the thin wings of linen oraria as ministering spirits sent out for service.

17. The embroidery on the arms of their robe shows the bonds of Christ: it is said that they bound Him and led Him to Caiaphas, the high priest, and to Pilate. The embroidery on the sides of their robe shows the blood which flowed for the side of Christ.

18. The epitrachilion is the cloth which was put on Christ at the hands of the high priest, and which was on His neck as He was bound and dragged to His passion.

19. The omophorion is like the stole of Aaron, which the priests of the (Old) Law wore, placing long cloths on their left shoulders. [The omophorion of the bishop is made of wool and not linen, for it represents the lost sheep which the Lord found and put upon His own shoulder.][10]

---

[10]This sentence is an extract from Letter I, 136, of Isidore of Pelusium.

Τὸ μοναχικὸν σχῆμά ἐστι κατὰ τὴν μίμησιν τοῦ
ἐρημοπολίτου καὶ βαπτιστοῦ Ἰωάννου ὅτι «ἦν τὸ
ἔνδυμα αὐτοῦ ἐκ τριχῶν καμήλου καὶ ζώνη δερμα-
τίνη περὶ τὴν ὀσφὺν αὐτοῦ». Ἔπειτα καὶ διὰ τὸ
πενθικὸν καὶ σκυθρωπὸν καὶ κατηφὲς καὶ ἐπίπονον
καὶ πρᾶον καὶ ταπεινὸν ἦθος τῶν τὸν μονήρη βίον
ἐπανηρημένων· πάντες γὰρ οἱ πενθοῦντες μέλανα πε-
ριβέβληνται καραδοκοῦντες ἀπολήψεσθαι τὴν λευκὴν
καὶ θείαν στολὴν τῆς δόξης τε καὶ παρακλήσεως τῆς
ἐν Χριστῷ Ἰησοῦ τῷ Κυρίῳ ἡμῶν.

Τὸ δὲ κείρεσθαι τὴν κάραν ὁλοτελῶς κατὰ τὴν
μίμησιν τοῦ ἁγίου ἀποστόλου Ἰακώβου· τοῦ ἀδελ-
φοθέου καὶ Παύλου τοῦ ἀποστόλου καὶ τῶν λοιπῶν.

Τὰ δὲ Ἀναβόλαιά εἰσι κατὰ τὰ ἀναβόλαια ἅπερ
ἐφόρουν ἱμάτια οἱ θεῖοι ἀπόστολοι.

Τὰ Κουκούλλια κατὰ τὸν λέγοντα ἀπόστολον
ὅτι «ἐσταύρωταί μοι ὁ κόσμος κἀγὼ τῷ κόσμῳ»· δι'
ὃ καὶ πορφυροῖς καὶ λευκοῖς λωρίοις καὶ σταυρίοις
κεκόσμηται διὰ τὸ ρυὲν ἐκ τῆς πλευρᾶς τοῦ Κυρίου
αἷμα καὶ ὕδωρ ὁμοῦ, ἐμφαίνοντα διὰ τῆς τοῦ μαντίου
ἀπολελυμένης ἁπλώσεως τὴν πτερωτικὴν τῆς τῶν
ἀγγέλων μιμήσεως· καθ' ὅτι ἀγγελικὸν σχῆμα λέγεται.

Ὁ . . . Ἀνάλαβος . . . δηλοῖ . . . τὸν ἀναλαβόντα
τὸν σταυρόν, καὶ τῇ πίστει κεκοσμημένον ἐνισχύεσθαι
περιφέροντα «τὸν θυρεὸν τῆς πίστεως ἐν ᾧ δυνήσεται
πάντα τὰ βέλη τὰ πεπυρωμένα τοῦ πονηροῦ σβέσαι,
καὶ τὴν περικεφαλαίαν τοῦ σωτηρίου δέξασθαι καὶ
τὴν μάχαιραν τοῦ Πνεύματος ὅ ἐστι ρῆμα Θεοῦ».

Τὸ δὲ ζώννυσθαι τὴν νέκρωσιν τοῦ σώματος δηλοῖ τοῦ τὴν σωφροσύνην περιφέροντος, περιεζῶσθαι
τὴν ὀσφὺν αὐτοῦ δύναμιν ἀληθείας.

The monastic schema is in imitation of the desert-dweller and Baptist John, whose cloak was of camel hair and the girdle about whose loins was of leather. This is also because of the grave, severe, sorrowful, suffering, humble, and poor way of life of those who enter upon the monastic way. For they all go into mourning and are dressed in black, expecting to receive the white, divine robe of glory and joy in Christ Jesus our Lord.

The total tonsuring of the head is in imitation of the holy Apostle James, brother of the Lord, and of the Apostle Paul, and of the rest.

The mantles are in the likeness of the mantles worn by the divine apostles.

The cowl is in accordance with the words of the apostle: "The world is crucified to me, and I to the world" (Gal 6:14). The purple and white embroidery and crosses which decorate it represent the blood and water flowing from the side of Christ, and the loosely unfolding mantle recalls the winged angels. Thus the schema is called angelic.

The scapular signifies him who takes up the cross and who, adorned with faith, is strengthened, wearing the shield of faith so as to be able to quench all the darts of the evil one and to accept the helmet of salvation and the sword of the spirit, which is the word of God (cf Ep 6:16-17).

The belt signifies that he wears the mortification of the body and chastity, having girded his loins with the power of truth.

Τὸ δὲ τοῖς Σανδαλίοις ἐπιβαίνειν αὐτὸν τῇ ὁδῷ τῆς σωτηρίας δηλοῖ τὸ ὅπως γένηται φοβερὸς τοῖς ὑπεναντίοις καὶ ἀνάλωτος τοῖς πολεμίοις «ὑποδεδεμένος τοὺς πόδας αὐτοῦ ἐν ἑτοιμασίᾳ τοῦ εὐαγγελίου τῆς εἰρήνης».

20. Ὁ ἄρτος τῆς προθέσεως, ἤγουν ὁ ἀποκαθαιρόμενος, ἐμφαίνει τὸν ὑπερβάλλοντα πλοῦτον τῆς χρηστότητος αὐτοῦ τοῦ Θεοῦ ἡμῶν ὅτι ὁ Υἱὸς τοῦ Θεοῦ ἄνθρωπος γέγονε, καὶ ἑαυτὸν προὔθηκε θυσίαν καὶ προσφορὰν εἰς ἀντίλυτρον καὶ ἐξίλασμα ὑπὲρ τῆς τοῦ κόσμου ζωῆς καὶ σωτηρίας· ἀναλαβὼν μὲν τὸ φύραμα ὅλον τῆς ἀνθρωπίνης φύσεως χωρὶς ἁμαρτίας, προσενεχθεὶς δὲ ὡς ἀπαρχὴ καὶ ἐξαίρετον ὁλοκάρπωμα τῷ Θεῷ καὶ Πατρὶ ὑπὲρ τοῦ ἀνθρωπείου φυράματος ὡς λέγεται· «Ἐγώ εἰμι ὁ ἄρτος ὁ ἐκ τοῦ οὐρανοῦ καταβάς» καί· «ὁ τρώγων τοῦτον τὸν ἄρτον ζήσεται εἰς τὸν αἰῶνα»· περὶ οὗ λέγει ὁ προφήτης Ἱερεμίας· «δεῦτε καὶ ἐμβάλωμεν ξύλον εἰς τὸν ἄρτον αὐτοῦ» δεικνὺς τὸ ξύλον τοῦ σταυροῦ τῷ σώματι ἐμπαγέν.

21. Τὸ δὲ ἐν τῇ λόγχῃ ἀποκείρεσθαι σημαίνει τό· «ὡς πρόβατον ἐπὶ σφαγὴν ἤχθη καὶ ὡς ἀμνὸς ἐναντίον τοῦ κείραντος αὐτὸν ἄφωνος».

22. Ὁ δὲ οἶνος καὶ τὸ ὕδωρ [ἐστὶ τὸ ἐξελθὸν ἐκ τῆς πλευρᾶς αὐτοῦ αἷμα καὶ ὕδωρ, καθὼς] ὁ προφήτης λέγει· «ἄρτος δοθήσεται αὐτῷ καὶ ὕδωρ αὐτοῦ ποτόν». Ἀντὶ γὰρ τῆς λόγχης τῆς κεντησάσης τὸν Χριστὸν ἐν τῷ σταυρῷ, ἐστὶ καὶ αὕτη ἡ λόγχη.

Ὁ Ἄρτος δὲ καὶ τὸ ποτήριον κυρίως καὶ ἀληθῶς, κατὰ μίμησιν τοῦ μυστικοῦ δείπνου, ἐν ᾧ ὁ Χριστὸς ἔλαβεν τὸν ἄρτον καὶ οἶνον καὶ εἶπε· «λάβετε, φάγετε καὶ πίετε πάντες· τοῦτό ἐστι τὸ σῶμά μου καὶ τὸ αἷμα» δεικνὺς ὅτι κοινωνοὺς ἡμᾶς ἐποίησε καὶ τοῦ θανάτου καὶ τῆς ἀναστάσεως αὐτοῦ καὶ δόξης.

And the sandals show his entering into the way of salvation so that he might become awesome to his adversaries and invincible to his enemies, and his feet are bound in preparation for the gospel of peace.

20. The bread of offering, that is to say, which is purified, signifies the superabundant riches of the goodness of our God, because the Son of God became man and gave Himself as an offering and oblation in ransom and atonement for the life and salvation of the world. He assumed the entirety of human nature, except for sin. He offered Himself as first-fruits and chosen whole burnt-offering to the God and Father on behalf of the human race, as is written: "I am the bread which came down from heaven," and "He who eats this bread will live for ever" (Jn 6:51). About this the Prophet Jeremiah says: "Come, let us place a stake in his bread" (11:19 LXX), pointing to the wood of the cross nailed to His body.

21. The piece which is cut out with the lance signifies that "Like a sheep he is led to the slaughter, and like a lamb that before its shearers is dumb" (cf Is 54:7).

22. The wine and the water are the blood and the water which came out from His side, as the prophet says: "Bread will be given him, and water to drink" (cf Is 33:16). For this lance corresponds to the lance which pierced Christ on the cross.

The bread and the chalice are really and truly the memorial of the mystical supper at which Christ, having taken the bread and wine, said: "Take, eat, and drink, all of you, this is my body and blood." This shows that He made us communicants of His death, His resurrection, and His glory.

Διὸ καὶ δεχόμενος ὁ ἱερεὺς ἐν κανισκίῳ παρὰ διακόνου ἢ ὑποδιακόνου τὴν προσφοράν, λαβών τε τὴν λόγχην καὶ ἀποκαθάρας αὐτήν, εἶτα σταυροειδῶς χαράξας αὐτὴν λέγει· «ὡς πρόβατον ἐπὶ σφαγὴν ἤχθη καὶ ὡς ἀμνὸς ἐναντίον τοῦ κείραντος αὐτὸν ἄφωνος», τοῦτο εἰπὼν λοιπὸν θεὶς τὴν αὐτὴν προσφορὰν ἐν τῷ ἁγίῳ δίσκῳ δακτυλοδείκτως ἐπάνω αὐτῆς φησὶν οὕτως· «οὕτως οὐκ ἀνοίγει τὸ στόμα αὐτοῦ, ἐν τῇ ταπεινώσει αὐτοῦ ἡ κρίσις αὐτοῦ ἤρθη, τὴν δὲ γενεὰν αὐτοῦ τίς διηγήσεται; ὅτι αἴρεται ἀπὸ τῆς γῆς ἡ ζωὴ αὐτοῦ». Διότι μετὰ τὸ εἰπεῖν ταῦτα λαβὼν τὸ ἅγιον ποτήριον, καὶ τοῦ διακόνου ἐπιχέοντος πάλιν εἰς αὐτὸ τὸν οἶνον καὶ τὸ ὕδωρ, πάλιν λέγει ὁ διάκονος· «ἐξῆλθεν ἐκ τῆς πλευρᾶς αὐτοῦ αἷμα καὶ ὕδωρ καὶ ὁ ἑωρακὼς μεμαρτύρηκε καὶ ἀληθινὴ ἐστιν ἡ μαρτυρία αὐτοῦ». Καὶ μετὰ ταῦτα θεὶς τὸ ἅγιον ποτήριον ἐν τῇ θείᾳ τραπέζῃ δακτυλοδεικτικῶς τε προσέχων τῷ σφαγιασθέντι ἀμνῷ διὰ τοῦ ἄρτου, καὶ κενωθέντι αἵματι διὰ τοῦ οἴνου, πάλιν λέγει ὅτι· «Τρεῖς εἰσιν οἱ μαρτυροῦντες, τὸ πνεῦμα καὶ τὸ ὕδωρ καὶ τὸ αἷμα, καὶ οἱ τρεῖς εἰς τὸ ἕν εἰσιν»· νῦν καὶ ἀεὶ καὶ εἰς τοὺς αἰῶνας.

Εἶτα λαβὼν τὸ θυμιατήριον καὶ θυμιάσας ποιεῖ εὐχὴν τῆς προθέσεως.

23. Τὰ Ἀντίφωνα τῆς λειτουργίας εἰσὶ τῶν προφητῶν αἱ προρρήσεις προκαταγγέλλουσαι τὴν παρουσίαν τοῦ Υἱοῦ τοῦ Θεοῦ, βοώντων· «ὁ Θεὸς ἡμῶν ἐπὶ τῆς γῆς ὤφθη καὶ τοῖς ἀνθρώποις συνανεστράφη»· καὶ «εὐπρέπειαν ἐνεδύσατο» ἤγουν τὴν σάρκωσιν αὐτοῦ δηλοῦντες, ἣν ἡμεῖς ἀποδεξάμενοι καὶ μαθόντες διὰ τῶν ὑπηρετῶν καὶ αὐτοπτῶν τοῦ Λόγου γενομένων διατόρως ταύτην ἀνακηρύττομεν.

24. Ἡ εἴσοδος τοῦ εὐαγγελίου ἐμφαίνει τὴν παρουσίαν καὶ τὴν εἴσοδον τοῦ Υἱοῦ τοῦ Θεοῦ εἰς τὸν κόσμον τοῦτον, καθώς φησιν ὁ ἀπόστολος· «ὅταν εἰσάγει, ἤγουν ὁ Θεὸς καὶ

Thus the priest takes the oblation, which is in a basket, from the deacon or the subdeacon. He takes the lance, cleanses it, then cutting the oblation in the form of a cross he says: "As a sheep led to the slaughter and as a lamb before its shearers is silent." Having said this, he places the oblation on the holy discos, points over it, saying: "He does not open His mouth: in His humility His judgment was taken away. Who will recount His generation? For His life is taken up from the earth." Having said these things, he takes the holy chalice and the deacon pours wine and water into it. Then the deacon says: "Blood and water poured from His side, and he who saw it has borne witness, and his witness is true." After this, he places the holy chalice on the divine table and, pointing at the bread, the sacrified lamb, and the wine, the blood poured out, says: "There are three who bear witness: the Spirit, the water, and the blood, and the three are one," (I Jn 5:8) now and ever and for the ages.

Then he takes the censer, adds incense, and says the prayer of the offering.

23. The antiphons of the liturgy are the prophecies of the prophets, foretelling the coming of the Son of God, proclaiming: "Our God has appeared upon earth and dwelt among men" (Bar 3:38) and "He is clothed in majesty" (Ps 92:1). The prophets are indicating His incarnation, of course, which we proclaim, having accepted and comprehended it through the ministers and eye-witnesses of the Word, who understood it.

24. The entrance of the Gospel signifies the coming of the Son of God and His entrance into this world, as the apostle says: "When He," that is the God and Father,

Πατήρ, τὸν πρωτότοκον εἰς τὴν οἰκουμένην λέγει· καὶ προσκυνησάτωσαν αὐτῷ πάντες οἱ ἄγγελοι αὐτοῦ». Ἔπειτα δεικνύντος τοῦ ἀρχιερέως διὰ τῆς στολῆς αὐτοῦ τὴν τῆς σαρκὸς τοῦ Χριστοῦ στολὴν τὴν ἐρυθρὰν καὶ αἱματώδη, ἣν ἐφόρεσεν ὁ ἄϋλος καὶ Θεός, ὡς πορφύραν βαφεῖσαν ἐξ ἀχράντων αἱμάτων τῆς θεοτόκου καὶ παρθένου· καὶ ἔλαβε τὸ πλανηθὲν πρόβατον ὁ ποιμὴν ὁ καλὸς ἐπὶ τῶν ὤμων αὐτοῦ, ἐν σπαργάνοις εἰληθεὶς καὶ τεθείς· οὐκ ἔστι ἐν φάτνῃ τῶν ἀλόγων ἀλλ' ἐν τραπέζῃ λογικῇ ἀνθρώπων λογικῶν· ὃν ὕμνησαν ἀγγέλων στρατιαὶ λέγουσαι· «δόξα ἐν ὑψίστοις Θεῷ καὶ ἐπὶ γῆς εἰρήνη ἐν ἀνθρώποις εὐδοκία»· καὶ «πᾶσα ἡ γῆ προσκυνησάτωσαν αὐτῷ»· Καὶ πάντων ἀνθυπακουόντων «δεῦτε προσκυνήσωμεν καὶ προσπέσωμεν· σῶσον ἡμᾶς Υἱὲ Θεοῦ»· καὶ κηρύττομεν τὴν παρουσίαν φανερωθεῖσαν ἡμῖν ἐν χάριτι Ἰησοῦ Χριστοῦ.

25. Ὁ τρισάγιος ὕμνος ἐστὶν οὕτως· ἐκεῖ μὲν ἄγγελοι εἶπον· «δόξα ἐν ὑψίστοις Θεῷ»· ἐνταῦθα δὲ ὡς οἱ μάγοι τὰ δῶρα ἡμεῖς προσφέροντες τῷ Χριστῷ, πίστιν, ἐλπίδα, ἀγάπην, ὡς χρυσὸν καὶ λίβανον καὶ σμύρναν, τῶν ἀσμάτων τὸ ἆσμα πιστῶς βοῶντες· ἅγιος ὁ Θεὸς ἤτοι ὁ πατήρ· ἅγιος ἰσχυρός, ὁ Υἱὸς καὶ Λόγος, διότι τὸν ἰσχυρὸν διάβολον δεσμεύσας κατήργησε διὰ σταυροῦ, τὸ κράτος ἔχοντα τοῦ θανάτου, καὶ τὴν ζωὴν ἡμῶν ἔδωκε τοῦ πατεῖν ἐπάνω αὐτοῦ· ἅγιος ἀθάνατος, τὸ Ἅγιον Πνεῦμα τὸ ζωοποιοῦν, δι' οὗ πᾶσα κτίσις ζωοποιεῖται καὶ βοᾷ· ἐλέησον ἡμᾶς.

Τὸ ἐκφωνῆσαι ἕνα τῶν ψαλτῶν ἐκ τοῦ ἄμβωνος προσέχοντα τῷ θυσιαστηρίῳ ἐν τῷ μέλλειν δοξάζειν μετὰ τὸν τριπλασιασμὸν τοῦ τρισαγίου καὶ λέγειν· «Εὐλογήσατε Κῦρι τὸ Δόξα», πληθυντικῶς, ἢ «Εὐλόγησον Κῦρι τὸ Δόξα», ἑνικῶς, τὸ μὲν (πληθυντικῶς) σημαίνει τὴν τρισυπόστατον μίαν θεότητα δέεσθαι ὡς ἐκ πάσης τῆς ἐκκλησίας εὐλογηθῆναι παρ' αὐτῆς (κατ' ἀξίαν) καθ' ὅσον ἐφικτὸν αὐτῇ ἀνθρώπῳ οὔσῃ καταξιωθῆναι σὺν ταῖς ἀσωμάτοις θείαις δυνάμεσιν

"brings the first-born into the world, He says: 'Let all God's angels worship him'" (Hb 1:6). Then the bishop, by his stole, manifests the red and bloody stole of the flesh of Christ. The immaterial One and God wore this stole, as porphyry decorated by the undefiled blood of the virgin Theotokos. The good shepherd took the lost sheep upon his shoulders: he is wrapped in swaddling clothes and placed not in a manger of irrational (animals), but on the rational table of rational men. The hosts of angels hymn him, saying: "Glory to God in the highest and peace on earth, good will to men" (Lk 2:14); and "Let all the earth worship Him" (Ps 65:4); and, heard by all: "Come let us worship and fall down before him: save us, O Son of God" (cf Ps 94:6). And we proclaim the coming which was revealed to us in the grace of Jesus Christ.

25. The Trisagion hymn is (sung) thus: there the angels say "Glory to God in the highest"; here, like the Magi, we bring gifts to Christ—faith, hope, and love like gold, frankincense, and myrrh—and like the bodiless hosts we cry in faith: "Holy God," that is the Father; "Holy Mighty," that is the Son and Word, for He has bound the mighty devil and made him who had dominion over death powerless through the cross and He has given us life by trampling on him; "Holy Immortal," that is the Holy Spirit, the giver of life, through whom all creation is made alive and cries out "Have mercy on us."

Then one of the psalmists on the ambo, facing the altar, about to say the "Glory" after the triple repetition of the Trisagion, says: "Bless (εὐλογή-σατε), master, the 'Glory,'" in the plural; or, in the singular: "Bless (εὐλόγησον), master, the 'Glory.'" The use of the singular represents the tri-hypostatic divine unity, as the whole church prays to be blessed by it insofar as it is possible for it, being human, to be counted worthy to sing the

τὸν χερουβικὸν καὶ τρισάγιον ὕμνον αὐτῇ τῇ ἁγίᾳ
Τριάδι ἀναμέλπειν· καὶ γὰρ διὰ τοῦ εἰπεῖν αὐτὸν
«εὐλογήσατε»· τὰς τρεῖς ὑποστάσεις. Πατρός, Υἱοῦ
καὶ Ἁγίου Πνεύματος ἐδήλωσεν, διὰ δὲ τοῦ προσ-
θεῖναι τὸ «Κῦρι» τὴν μίαν φύσιν τῆς θεότητος ἐτρά-
νωσεν.

26. Τὸ ἀνελθεῖν ἐν τῷ συνθρόνῳ τὸν ἀρχιερέα καὶ
σφραγίσαι τὸν λαόν, ἐστὶν ὁ Υἱὸς τοῦ Θεοῦ ὅτε ἐπλήρωσε
τὴν οἰκονομίαν, ἐπάρας τὰς χεῖρας αὐτοῦ εὐλόγησε τοὺς
ἁγίους αὐτοῦ μαθητὰς λέγων αὐτοῖς· «εἰρήνην ἀφίημι ὑμῖν»
δεικνύων ὅτι τὴν αὐτὴν εἰρήνην καὶ εὐλογίαν ἔδωκε τῷ
κόσμῳ ὁ Χριστὸς διὰ τῶν ἀποστόλων αὐτοῦ.

Τὸ δὲ «καὶ τῷ πνεύματί σου» παρὰ τοῦ λαοῦ ἀπο-
κρινόμενον τοῦτο δηλοῖ ὅτι, εἰρήνην μὲν παρέσχες,
Κύριε, τὴν ἐν ἀλλήλοις ὁμόνοιαν, εἰρήνην δὲ δὸς
ἡμῖν τὴν πρὸς σὲ ἀδιαίρετον ἔνωσιν· ἵνα τῷ πνεύματί
σου εἰρηνεύοντες ὃ ἡμῖν ἐν ἀρχῇ τῆς δημιουργίας
[σου] ἐνέθηκας, ἀχώριστοι τῆς σῆς ἀγάπης τυγχά-
νωμεν.

27. Τὸ δὲ καθίσαι ἐστὶν ὅτε ὁ Υἱὸς τοῦ Θεοῦ τὴν
σάρκα [ἢν ἐφό]ρεσε καὶ τὸ πρόβατον ὃ ἀνέλαβεν ἐπὶ τῶν
ὤμων, ὅπερ σημαίνει τὸ ὠμοφόριον ὅ ἐστι τὸ ἀδαμιαῖον φύραμα ἀνεβίβασεν αὐτὴν ὑπεράνω πάσης ἀρχῆς καὶ ἐξουσίας
καὶ κυριότητος τῶν ἄνω δυνάμεων, καὶ προσήγαγεν αὐτὴν
τῷ Θεῷ καὶ Πατρί. [Ἐπειδὴ γὰρ ὃ μὲν ἐθέωσε, ὃ δὲ ἐθε-
ώθη, τουτέστι τὸ πρόσλημμα ὃ διὰ τὴν ἀξίαν τοῦ προσενέγ-
καντος καὶ τὴν καθαρότητα τοῦ προσενεχθέντος], ἐδέξατο
αὐτὸ ὁ Θεὸς καὶ Πατὴρ ὡς θυσίαν καὶ προσφορὰν εὐάρεστον

Cherubicon and the Trisagion, along with the in-
corporeal, divine powers, to the Holy Trinity itself.
When he says "Bless" in the plural, he signifies
the three hypostases, of the Father, Son, and Holy
Spirit, and when he adds "Master," he expresses
the one nature of the divinity.

26. The ascent of the bishop to the throne and his
blessing the people signifies that the Son of God, having
completed the economy of salvation, raised his hands
and blessed His holy disciples, saying to them: "Peace I
leave with you" (Jn 14:27). This shows that Christ gave
the same peace and blessing to the world through His
disciples.

And the "And with your spirit" by which the
people respond signifies that You conferred peace,
O Lord, which is mutual concord: You gave us
peace which is for indivisible union with You, so
that being at peace through Your Spirit, whom
You gave us at the beginning of [Your] creation,
we might become inseparable from Your love.[11]

27. The sitting represents the time when the Son of
God raised His body [which He wore] and the sheep
which He put upon His shoulder—that is the nature of
Adam, which is represented by the omophorion—above any
beginning, power, or authority of the higher powers, and
brought it to His God and Father. [And because the One
deifies, and the other is deified, that is the assumed humanity, because of the holiness of the offerer and the
purity of the offered], God the Father Himself received
it as a sacrifice and as an acceptable offering on behalf of
the human race. About the Son it is said: ["The Lord

---

[11]Extract from Letter I, 122, of Isidore of Pelusium.

ὑπὲρ τοῦ ἀνθρωπείου γένους, πρὸς ὃν καὶ εἶπεν· «[εἶπεν ὁ Κύριος τῷ Κυρίῳ μου», ἤτοι ὁ Πατὴρ πρὸς τὸν Υἱόν], «κάθου ἐκ δεξιῶν μου», ὃς καὶ ἐκάθισεν ἐν δεξιᾷ τοῦ θρόνου τῆς μεγαλωσύνης ἐν τοῖς ὑψηλοῖς. [Οὗτος ἐστιν Ἰησοῦς ὁ Ναζωραῖος ὁ ἀρχιερεὺς τῶν μελλόντων ἀγαθῶν].

28. Τὸ προκείμενον μηνύει πάλιν τὴν τῶν προφητῶν ἐκφαντορίαν καὶ προμήνυσιν τῆς τοῦ Χριστοῦ παρουσίας· ὡς στρατιῶται προτρέχοντες καὶ βοῶντες· «ὁ καθήμενος ἐπὶ τῶν χερουβὶμ ἐμφάνηθι καὶ ἐλθὲ εἰς τὸ σῶσαι ἡμᾶς»· [καὶ «ὁ Θεὸς κάθηται ἐπὶ θρόνου ἁγίου αὐτοῦ»].

Ὁ ἀπόστολος καὶ αὐτόπτης καὶ ὑπουργὸς τοῦ Χριστοῦ βοᾷ κηρύσσων τὴν βασιλείαν τοῦ Χριστοῦ λέγων· «Χριστὸς παραγενόμενος ἀρχιερεὺς τῶν μελλόντων ἀγαθῶν, ὃν (καὶ) ἔχοντες ἀρχιερέα μέγαν διεληλυθότα τοὺς οὐρανοὺς κρατῶμεν τῆς ὁμολογίας» αὐτοῦ, μεθ᾽ οὗ βοᾷ καὶ Ἰωάννης ὁ βαπτιστής· Ὁ ὀπίσω μου ἐρχόμενός ἐστιν ὁ «ἀμνὸς τοῦ Θεοῦ ὁ αἴρων τὴν ἁμαρτίαν τοῦ κόσμου· αὐτὸς ἡμᾶς ἁγιάσει ἐν πνεύματι (ἁγίῳ) καὶ πυρὶ (καὶ) μέσον ὑμῶν ἔστηκε».

29. [Τὸ ἀλληλούϊα βοᾷ Δαβὶδ καὶ λέγει· «ὁ Θεὸς ἡμῶν ἐμφανῶς ἥξει καὶ πῦρ ἐνώπιον αὐτοῦ προπορεύσεται, ἔφαναν αἱ ἀστραπαὶ τῶν εὐαγγελιστῶν αὐτοῦ τῇ οἰκουμένῃ»]. Τὸ δὲ ἀλληλούϊα τῇ ἑβραΐδι διαλέκτῳ ἐστὶν τὸ ΑΛ ἔρχεται, ἐφάνη· τὸ ΗΛ ὁ Θεός, τὸ δὲ ΟΥΙΑ αἰνεῖτε, ὑμνεῖτε, τὸν ζῶντα Θεόν.

30. Ὁ θυμιατὴρ δεικνύει τὴν ἀνθρωπότητα τοῦ Χριστοῦ· τὸ πῦρ τὴν θεότητα, ὁ εὐώδης καπνὸς μηνύει τὴν εὐωδίαν τοῦ Ἁγίου Πνεύματος προπορευομένην· ὁ γὰρ θυμιατὴρ ἑρμηνεύεται εὐωδεστάτη εὐφροσύνη.

Ἢ πάλιν ἡ γαστὴρ τοῦ θυμιατηρίου νοηθείη

says to my Lord," that is the Father to the Son], "Sit at
my right hand" (Ps 109:1), and He sat on the right hand
of the throne of majesty in the highest heaven. [This is
Jesus the Nazarene, high priest of the good things to
come.]

28. The prokeimenon again indicates the revelation
and prophecy of the prophets about the coming of Christ.
Like soldiers they run ahead and shout: "You who sit
upon the Cherubim, appear and come to save us" [and
"God sits upon His holy throne"].

The apostle, eyewitness and minister of Christ,
proclaiming the Kingdom of Christ, exclaims, saying: "Christ appeared as a high priest of the good
things to come" (Hb 9:11). "Having a great high
priest who has passed through the heavens, let us
hold fast in professing him." With Paul, John the
Baptist also exclaims: "He who comes after me
is 'the lamb of God, who takes away the sin of
the world!' (Jn 1:29) He sanctified us in the (Holy)
Spirit and fire, and stood among you."

29. [David exclaims alleluia and says: "Our God will
come clearly and fire shall go before Him" (Ps 49:3). The
brightness of His evangelists has shone through the world.]
For in Hebrew AL means "He comes, He appears"; EL
means "God"; and OUIA means "praise and sing hymns"
to the living God.

30. The censer demonstrates the humanity of Christ,
and the fire, His divinity. The sweet-smelling smoke reveals the fragrance of the Holy Spirit which precedes. For
the censer denotes sweet joy.

Again, the interior of the censer is understood

ἂν (ἡμῖν) ἡ (ἡγιασμένη) μήτρα τῆς (ἁγίας) παρθένου (καὶ θεοτόκου) φοροῦσα τὸν θεῖον ἄνθρακα
Χριστόν, «ἐν ᾧ κατοικεῖ πᾶν τὸ πλήρωμα τῆς θεότητος σωματικῶς», διὸ καὶ τὴν ὀσμὴν τῆς εὐωδίας
ἀναδίδωσιν εὐωδιάζων τὰ σύμπαντα· ἢ πάλιν ἡ γαστὴρ τοῦ θυμιατηρίου δηλοῖ τὴν κολυμβήθραν τοῦ
ἁγίου βαπτίσματος· ἐν ἄνθρακι τοῦ θείου πυρὸς τῆς
τοῦ Ἁγίου Πνεύματος ἐνεργείας τὴν εὐώδη τῆς
θείας χάριτος υἱοθεσίαν διὰ τῆς πίστεως ἑαυτῇ εἰσοι-
κίζουσα καὶ δι᾽ αὐτῆς εὐωδιάζουσα.

31. Τὸ εὐαγγέλιόν ἐστιν ἡ παρουσία τοῦ Θεοῦ καθ᾽
ἣν ὡράθη ἡμῖν, οὐκ ἔτι διὰ νεφελῶν καὶ αἰνιγμάτων λαλῶν
ἡμῖν ὥς ποτε τῷ Μωϋσῇ διὰ φωνῶν καὶ ἀστραπῶν καὶ
σαλπίγγων ἤχῳ καὶ γνόφῳ καὶ πυρὶ ἐπὶ τοῦ ὄρους, ἢ τοῖς
προφήταις δι᾽ ἐνυπνίων, ἀλλ᾽ ἐμφανῶς ὡς ἄνθρωπος ἀληθινὸς ἐφάνη καὶ ὡράθη ἡμῖν ὁ πραΰς καὶ ἥσυχος βασιλεὺς
ὁ πρὶν καταβὰς ἀφοφητὶ ἐν πόκῳ· «καὶ ἐθεασάμεθα τὴν δόξαν αὐτοῦ, δόξαν ὡς μονογενοῦς πλήρης χάριτος καὶ ἀληθείας», δι᾽ οὗ ἐλάλησεν ἡμῖν ὁ Θεὸς καὶ Πατὴρ στόμα πρὸς
στόμα καὶ οὐ δι᾽ αἰνιγμάτων, περὶ οὗ ὁ Πατὴρ ἐξ οὐρανοῦ
μαρτυρεῖ καὶ λέγει· «οὗτός ἐστιν ὁ Υἱός μου ὁ ἀγαπητός»,
σοφία, λόγος καὶ δύναμις, ὁ ἐν προφήταις μὲν κηρυχθεὶς
ἡμῖν· ἐν εὐαγγελίοις δὲ φανερωθεὶς ἵνα «ὅσοι λάβωσιν αὐτὸν
καὶ πιστεύουσιν εἰς τὸ ὄνομα αὐτοῦ λάβωσιν ἐξουσίαν τέκνα
Θεοῦ γενέσθαι». Ὃν ἀκηκόαμεν καὶ «ἑωράκαμεν τοῖς ὀφθαλ-
μοῖς ἡμῶν», σοφίαν καὶ λόγον Θεοῦ τοῦτον εἶναι πάντες βο-
ῶμεν· δόξα σοι κύριε. Εἶτα πάλιν τὸ Ἅγιον Πνεῦμα βοᾷ τὸ
ἐν νεφέλῃ φωτεινῇ ἐπισκιάζον, νῦν δι᾽ ἀνθρώπου βοᾷ· προσέ-
χετε, «αὐτοῦ ἀκούετε».

32. Τέσσαρα δὲ εὐαγγέλιά εἰσιν, ἐπειδὴ τέσσαρα καθο-
λικὰ πνεύματά εἰσι κατὰ τὰ τετράμορφα ζῶα ἐν οἷς κάθηται

as the [sanctified] womb of the [holy] virgin [and
Theotokos] who bore the divine coal, Christ, in
whom "the whole fulness of deity dwells bodily"
(Col 2:9). All together, therefore, give forth the
sweet-smelling fragrance. Or again, the interior of
the censer points to the font of holy baptism,
taking into itself the coal of divine fire, the sweet-
ness of the operation of the Holy Spirit, which is
the adoption of divine grace through faith, and
exuding a good odor.

31. The Gospel is the coming of God, when He was
seen by us: He is no longer speaking to us as through a
cloud and indistinctly, as He did to Moses through thunder
and lightning and trumpets, by a voice, by darkness and
fire on the mountain. Nor does He appear through dreams
as to the prophets, but He appeared visibly as a true
man. He was seen by us as a gentle and peaceful king
who descended quietly like rain upon the fleece, and we
have beheld His glory, glory as of the only-begotten Son,
full of grace and truth (cf Jn 1:14). Through Him, the
God and Father spoke to us face to face, and not through
riddles. From heaven the Father bears witness to Him,
saying "This is my beloved Son" (Mt 3:17), wisdom, word,
and power, who is foretold to us by the prophets. He is
revealed in the gospels, so that all who receive Him and
believe in His name might receive the power to become
children of God (cf Jn 1:12). We have heard and seen
with our eyes that He is the wisdom and word of God,
and we all cry "Glory to You, O Lord." And the Holy
Spirit, who was concealed in a bright cloud, now exclaims through a man: "Attend, listen to Him."

32. There are four gospels because there are four
universal winds, corresponding to the four-formed crea-

ὁ τῶν ὅλων Θεός, καὶ συνέχων τὰ σύμπαντα φανερωθεὶς ἔδω-
κεν ἡμῖν τετράμορφον τὸ εὐαγγέλιον, ἑνὶ δὲ πνεύματι συν-
ερχόμενον· καὶ γὰρ τετραπρόσωπά εἰσι, καὶ τὰ πρόσωπα
αὐτῶν εἰκονίζουσι τὴν πραγματείαν τοῦ Υἱοῦ τοῦ Θεοῦ. Τὸ
μὲν γὰρ πρῶτον ὅμοιον λέοντι τὸ ἔμπρακτον αὐτοῦ καὶ ἡγε-
μονικὸν καὶ βασιλικὸν χαρακτηρίζον· τὸ δεύτερον ὅμοιον
μόσχῳ, τὴν ἱερουργικὴν καὶ ἱερατικὴν ἐμφαῖνον· τὸ δὲ τρίτον
ἔχον πρόσωπον ἀνθρώπου, τὴν κατὰ ἄνθρωπον αὐτοῦ παρουσίαν φανερῶς διαγράφον· τὸ δὲ τέταρτον ὅμοιον ἀετῷ πετο-
μένῳ, τὴν διὰ τοῦ Ἁγίου Πνεύματος δόσιν σαφηνίζον. Καὶ
τὰ εὐαγγέλια τούτοις σύμμορφά εἰσιν ἐν οἷς κάθηται ὁ Χρι-
στός· τὸ μὲν γὰρ κατὰ Ἰωάννην εὐαγγέλιον τὴν ἀπὸ τοῦ
Πατρὸς ἡγεμονικὴν αὐτοῦ καὶ πατρικὴν καὶ ἔνδοξον γέννησιν διηγεῖται· τὸ δὲ κατὰ Λουκᾶν ἅτε ἱερατικοῦ χαρακτῆ-
ρος ὑπάρχον, ἀπὸ τοῦ Ζαχαρίου ἱερέως θυμιῶντος ἐν τῷ ναῷ
ἄρχεται. Ματθαῖος δὲ τὴν κατὰ ἄνθρωπον αὐτό, διηγεῖται
γέννησιν «Βίβλος γενέσεως»· ἀνθρωπόμορφον οὖν τὸ εὐαγγέλιον τοῦτο. Μάρκος δὲ ἀπὸ τοῦ προφητικοῦ πνεύματος, ἐξ
ὕψους ἐπιόντος τοῖς ἀνθρώποις, τὴν ἀρχὴν ἐποιήσατο λέ-
γων· «Ἀρχὴ τοῦ εὐαγγελίου Ἰησοῦ Χριστοῦ ὡς γέγραπται
ἐν τοῖς προφήταις· ἰδοὺ ἐγὼ ἀποστελῶ τὸν ἄγγελόν μου»,
τὴν πτερωτικὴν εἰκόνα τοῦ εὐαγγελίου δεικνύς.

33. Τὸ κατασφραγίσαι τὸν ἀρχιερέα τὸν λαόν, ὑποδεικνύει τὴν μέλλουσαν παρουσίαν τοῦ Χριστοῦ ἐν ͵ςφ΄ ἔτει
μέλλειν ἔσεσθαι διὰ τῆς ψήφου τῶν δακτύλων ἐμφαινού-
σης ͵ςφ΄.

34. Τὸ εἰλητὸν σημαίνει τὴν σινδόνα ἣ ἐνηλίθη ὁ

tures[12] on which the God of all sits. Holding them all together, and having been revealed, He gave us the four-
formed gospel, which is joined together by one Spirit. And
they have four faces, and their faces represent the activity
of the Son of God. For the first resembles a lion, charac-
terizing His activity, authority, and royalty. The second
resembles a calf, manifesting His holy work and priesthood. The third has the face of a man, which clearly
delineates His coming as a man. And the fourth resembles
a flying eagle, explaining the gift of the Holy Spirit. And
the gospels correspond to these four animals, on which
Christ sits. For the Gospel of John recounts His sovereign,
paternal, and glorious birth from His Father. The Gospel
of Luke, being of priestly character, begins with the priest
Zachariah burning incense in the temple. Matthew tells
about His birth according to His humanity—"the book
of the genealogy." Therefore this gospel is in the form
of a man. And Mark begins from the prophetic spirit,
which comes to men from on high, making the beginning
say: "The beginning of the gospel of Jesus Christ, as it is
written in the prophets: 'Behold, I send my messenger' "
(Mk 1:1-2). It thus points to the winged image of the
gospel.

33. When the bishop blesses the people, it indicates
the second coming of Christ in 6,500 years, as shown
by the fingers "ϛφ."[13]

34. The eiliton[14] signifies the winding sheet in which

---

[12]The beasts which surround the throne of God in Rv 4:7-8
and Is 6:2-3. See also ch 41 below.

[13]The Byzantines were fond of ascribing various symbolic meanings to the manner in which the fingers were held for blessing.
Several are described in the *Dictionnaire d'Archéologie Chrétienne
et de Liturgie* II, pt. 2, 752-755. This particular interpretation is
not clear.

[14]A large cloth which was placed on the altar before the deposition of the gifts.

Χριστὸς τὸ σῶμα ἐκ τοῦ σταυροῦ καταβὰς καὶ ἐν μνημείῳ τεθείς.

35. Οἱ κατηχούμενοι ἐξέρχονται ὡς ἀμύητοι τοῦ θείου βαπτίσματος καὶ τῶν τοῦ Χριστοῦ μυστηρίων, περὶ ὧν λέγει ὁ Κύριος· «καὶ ἄλλα πρόβατα ἔχω, κἀκεῖνά με δεῖ ἀγαγεῖν καὶ τῆς φωνῆς μου ἀκούσουσιν (καὶ γενήσεται μία ποίμνη εἷς ποιμήν)».

36. Ἡ προσκομιδὴ ἡ γενομένη ἐν τῷ θυσιαστηρίῳ, ἤτοι ἐν τῷ σκευοφυλακίῳ, ἐμφαίνει τοῦ κρανίου τὸν τόπον ἐν ᾧ ἐσταυρώθη ὁ Χριστός· ἐν ᾧ λόγος (ἐστὶ) κεῖσθαι τὸ κρανίον τοῦ προπάτορος ἡμῶν Ἀδάμ, δείκνυσι δὲ ὅτι «ἐγγὺς ἦν τὸ μνημεῖον ὅπου ἐσταυρώθη». Προετυπώθη δὲ ὁ κρανὸς οὗτος ἐν τῷ Ἀβραὰμ ὅτε ἐφ᾽ ἑνὶ τῶν ὀρέων ἐκείνων, τοῦ Θεοῦ κελεύσαντος, τὸ θυσιαστήριον ἐκ λίθων ἐποίησε καὶ ἐστίβασε ξύλα καὶ ἔθηκε τὸν υἱόν· καὶ ἀνήνεγκε κριὸν ἀντ᾽ αὐτοῦ εἰς ὁλοκάρπωσιν. Οὕτω καὶ ὁ Θεὸς καὶ Πατὴρ ὁ ἄναρχος καὶ παλαιὸς τῶν ἡμερῶν τὸν ἄναρχον (sic) αὐτοῦ Υἱὸν (εὐδόκησε) ἐπ᾽ ἐσχάτων τῶν χρόνων σαρκωθῆναι ἐξ ἀχράντου θεοτόκου παρθένου ἐκ τῆς ὀσφύος αὐτοῦ (Ἀβραὰμ) κατ᾽ ἐπαγγελίαν ὅρκου οὗ ἔθηκε πρὸς αὐτόν, ἔπαθε δὲ ὡς ἄνθρωπος τῇ σαρκὶ αὐτοῦ, ἀλλ᾽ ἔμεινεν ἀπαθὴς θεότητι· καὶ γὰρ ὁ Χριστὸς ἀπερχόμενος ἐν τῷ σταυρῷ αὐτοῦ, τὸν σταυρὸν αὐτοῦ ἐβάστασε, καὶ ἀντὶ κριοῦ ἐτύθη τὸ σῶμα αὐτοῦ τὸ ἄμωμον, ὡς ἀμνὸς σφαττόμενος τῇ λόγχῃ τὴν πλευρὰν αὐτοῦ, καὶ ἀρχιερεὺς γενόμενος καὶ προσφέρων ἑαυτὸν καὶ προσφερόμενος εἰς τὸ ἀνενέγκαι ἁμαρτίας πολλῶν, καὶ τέθνηκεν ὡς

the body of Christ was wrapped when it was taken down
from the cross and placed in a tomb.

35. The catechumens go out because they are un-
initiated into the baptism of God and the mysteries of
Christ. About the catechumens the Lord says: "And I
have other sheep; I must bring them also, and they will
heed my voice. [So there shall be one flock, one shepherd]"
(cf Jn 10:16).

36. The proskomedē,[15] which takes place on the
altar located in the skeuophylakion,[16] signifies the place
of Calvary, where Jesus was crucified. There, it is said,
lies the skull of our forefather Adam, and it is pointed
out that "there was a tomb near to where He was crucified"
(cf Jn 19:41-42). This Calvary was prefigured by Abraham
when he, commanded by God, made an altar of stone on
one of those mountains, collected wood, and placed his
son on it, and then offered a ram instead as a burnt-
offering. Thus the God and Father, Who is without beginning and ancient of days, was pleased for His eternal
Son to be incarnate in the last times from the undefiled
virgin Theotokos from the loins of Adam, according to a
vowed promise which He made him. And as a man He suf-
fered in the flesh, but in His divinity He remained impas-
sible. For Christ, going forth to His crucifixion, took up His
cross and offered His own blameless body instead of a ram,
as a lamb pierced in the side with a spear. And He became
a high priest, offering Himself and offered in order to bear
the sins of many. He died as a man and rose as God, and
thereby He obtained that glory [which He had] before

---

[15]The preparation of elements.

[16]A round building located near the NE corner of Hagia
Sophia, where the precious vessels and vestments were kept, where
people brought their gifts prior to the liturgy, and where the
preparation of the elements took place.

ἄνθρωπος, ἀνέστη δὲ ὡς Θεὸς δι᾽ ἣν εἶχε πρὸ κόσμου δόξαν παρὰ Θεῷ καὶ γεννήτορι.

37. Ὁ χερουβικὸς ὕμνος διὰ τῆς τῶν διακόνων προοδοποιήσεως καὶ τῆς τῶν ρυπίδων σεραφικῶν ἀπεικονισμάτων ἱστορίας, τὴν εἴσοδον τῶν ἁγίων καὶ δικαίων ἁπάντων συνεισερχομένων ἔμπροσθεν τῶν χερουβικῶν δυνάμεων, καὶ ἀγγελικῶν στρατιῶν ἀοράτως προτρεχουσῶν τοῦ μεγάλου βασιλέως Χριστοῦ προσερχομένου εἰς μυστικὴν θυσίαν καὶ ὑπὸ χειρῶν ἐνύλων βασταζομένου, μεθ᾽ ὧν τὸ Πνεῦμα τὸ Ἅγιον εἰσπορεύεται ἔμπροσθεν ἐν τῇ ἀναιμάκτῳ καὶ λογικῇ θυσίᾳ νοερῶς θεωρούμενον, πυρὶ καὶ θυμιάματι καὶ ἀτμίδι καὶ πνεύματι εὐώδους· τοῦ μὲν πυρὸς δεικνύοντος τὴν θεότητα, τοῦ δὲ εὐώδους καπνοῦ τὴν παρουσίαν αὐτοῦ ἐπελθόντος ἀοράτως καὶ εὐωδιάσαντος ἡμᾶς διὰ τῆς μωστικῆς καὶ ζωοθύτου καὶ ἀναιμάκτου λατρείας καὶ ὁλοκαρπώσεως. Ἀλλὰ καὶ αἱ νοεραὶ δυνάμεις καὶ αἱ χοροστασίαι τῶν ἀγγέλων ὁρῶσαι τὴν διὰ σταυροῦ καὶ θανάτου τοῦ Χριστοῦ τελεσιουργουμένην αὐτοῦ οἰκονομίαν καὶ τὴν κατὰ τοῦ θανάτου νίκην γενομένην καὶ τὴν ἐν τῷ ᾅδῃ κάθοδον καὶ τριήμερον ἀνάστασιν σὺν ἡμῖν βοῶσιν τὸ Ἀλληλούια.

Ἔστι καὶ κατὰ μίμησιν τοῦ ἐνταφιασμοῦ τοῦ Χριστοῦ, καθ᾽ ἣν ὁ Ἰωσὴφ καθελὼν τὸ σῶμα ἀπὸ τοῦ σταυροῦ ἐνείλισσε σινδόνι καθαρᾷ καὶ ἀρώμασι καὶ μύροις αὐτὸ ἀλείψας, ἐβάστασε σὺν Νικοδήμῳ καὶ ἐκήδευσεν ἐν τῷ μνημείῳ τῷ καινῷ τῷ λελατομημένῳ ἐκ πέτρας. Ἔστι δὲ ἀντίτυπον τοῦ ἁγίου μνήματος τὸ θυσιαστήριον καὶ τὸ καταθέσιον, δηλαδὴ ἐν ᾧ ἐτέθη τὰ ἄχραντον καὶ πανάγιον σῶμα, ἡ θεία τράπεζα.

38. Δίσκος ἐστὶν ἀντὶ τῶν χειρῶν Ἰωσὴφ καὶ Νικοδήμου τῶν κηδευσάντων τὸν Χριστόν. Ἑρμηνεύεται δὲ δίσκος καὶ ὅπερ ἐπιφέρεται ὁ Χριστὸς κύκλον οὐρανοῦ, ἐμφαίνων ἡμῖν ἐν μικρᾷ περιγραφῇ τὸν νοητὸν ἥλιον Χριστὸν χωρῶν ἐν τῷ ἄρτῳ καὶ ὁρώμενος.

39. Τὸ δὲ ποτήριόν ἐστι ἀντὶ τοῦ σκεύους οὗ ἐδέξατο

the world together with [His] God and Begettor (cf Hb 7:26-28).

37. By means of the procession of the deacons and the representation of the fans, which are in the likeness of the seraphim, the Cherubic Hymn signifies the entrance of all the saints and righteous ahead of the cherubic powers and the angelic hosts, who run invisibly in advance of the great king, Christ, who is proceeding to the mystical sacrifice, borne aloft by material hands. Together with them comes the Holy Spirit in the unbloody and reasonable sacrifice. The Spirit is seen spiritually in the fire, incense, smoke, and fragrant air: for the fire points to His divinity, and the fragrant smoke to His coming invisibly and filling us with good fragrance through the mystical, living, and unbloody service and sacrifice of burnt-offering. In addition, the spiritual powers and the choirs of angels, who have seen His dispensation fulfilled through the cross and death of Christ, the victory over death which has taken place, the descent into hell and the resurrection on the third day, with us exclaim the alleluia.

It is also in imitation of the burial of Christ, when Joseph took down the body from the cross, wrapped it in clean linen, anointed it with spices and ointment, carried it with Nicodemus, and placed it in a new tomb hewn out of a rock. The altar is an image of the holy tomb, and the divine table is the sepulchre in which, of course, the undefiled and all-holy body was placed.

38. The discos represents the hands of Joseph and Nicodemus, who buried Christ. The discos on which Christ is carried is also interpreted as the sphere of heaven, manifesting to us in miniature the spiritual sun, Christ, and containing Him visibly in the bread.

39. The chalice corresponds to the vessel which re-

τὸ ἐκβλύσαν τῆς αἱμαχθείσης ἀχράντου πλευρᾶς καὶ χειρῶν καὶ ποδῶν τοῦ Χριστοῦ ἀπομύρισμα. Τὸ ποτήριον δὲ πάλιν ἐστὶν κατὰ τὸν κρατῆρα ὃν γράφει ὁ Κύριος, ἤτοι ἡ σοφία, ὅτι ὁ Υἱὸς τοῦ Θεοῦ ἐκέρασε τὸ αἷμα αὐτοῦ ἀντὶ τοῦ οἴνου ἐκείνου, καὶ προέθηκεν ἐν τῇ ἁγίᾳ τραπέζῃ αὐτοῦ λέγων τοῖς πᾶσι· Πίετε τὸ αἷμά μου κεκερασμένον ὑμῖν εἰς ἄφεσιν ἁμαρτιῶν καὶ εἰς ζωὴν αἰώνιον.

40. Τὸ δισκοκάλυμμά ἐστιν ἀντὶ τοῦ σουδαρίου οὗ ἦν ἐπὶ τῆς κεφαλῆς καὶ τοῦ προσώπου τοῦ Χριστοῦ περικαλύπτον αὐτὸ ἐν τάφῳ.

41. Τὸ καταπέτασμα, ἤγουν ὁ ἀήρ, ἐστὶν ἀντὶ τοῦ λίθου οὗ ἐσφάλισε τὸ μνημεῖον ὁ Ἰωσὴφ ὅνπερ καὶ ἐσφράγισεν ἡ τοῦ Πιλάτου κουστωδία.

Τὸ καταπέτασμα λέγεται διὰ τὸν λέγοντα Ἀπόστολον ὅτι «ἔχομεν παρρησίαν εἰς τὴν εἴσοδον τῶν ἁγίων ἐν τῷ αἵματι Ἰησοῦ Χριστοῦ ἣν ἐνεκαίνισεν ἡμῖν ὁδὸν πρόσφατον καὶ ζῶσαν διὰ τοῦ καταπετάσματος, τουτέστι τῆς σαρκὸς αὐτοῦ, καὶ ἱερέα μέγαν ἐπὶ τὸν οἶκον τοῦ Θεοῦ».

Ἰδοὺ ἐσταύρωται ὁ Χριστός, τέθαπται ἡ ζωή, ἐσφαλίσθη ὁ τάφος, ἐσφραγίσθη ὁ λίθος· πρόσεισιν ὁ ἱερεύς, συνέρχεται ταῖς ἀγγελικαῖς δυνάμεσιν, οὐκέτι ὡς ἐν ἐπιγείῳ ἑστώς, ἀλλ᾽ ὡς ἐν τῷ ἐπουρανίῳ θυσιαστηρίῳ, ἔμπροσθεν τοῦ θυσιαστηρίου τοῦ θρόνου τοῦ Θεοῦ παριστάμενος θεωρεῖ τὸ μέγα καὶ ἀνερμήνευτον καὶ ἀνεξιχνίαστον τοῦ Θεοῦ μυστήριον· ὁμολογεῖ τὴν χάριν, κηρύττει τὴν ἀνάστασιν, σφραγίζει τὴν πίστιν τῆς ἁγίας Τριάδος. Πρόσεισι λευχειμονῶν ὁ ἄγγελος

ceived the mixture which poured out from the bloodied, undefiled side and from the hands and feet of Christ. Or again, the chalice corresponds to the bowl which the Lord depicts, that is, Wisdom; because the Son of God has mixed His blood for drinking instead of that wine, and set it forth on His holy table, saying to all: "Drink of my blood mixed for you for the remission of sins and eternal life."

40. The cover on the discos corresponds to the cloth which was on Christ's head and which covered His face in the tomb.

41. The veil, or the aer, corresponds to the stone which Joseph placed against the tomb and which the guards of Pilate sealed.

> The apostle speaks thus about the veil: "We have confidence to enter the sanctuary by the blood of Jesus Christ, by the new and living way He opened to us through the veil, that is through His flesh, and since we have a great priest over the house of God" (Cf Hb 10:19-21).

Thus Christ is crucified, life is buried, the tomb is secured, the stone is sealed. In the company of the angelic powers, the priest[17] approaches, standing no longer as on earth, but attending at the heavenly altar, before the altar of the throne of God, and he contemplates the great, ineffable, and unsearchable mystery of God. He gives thanks, proclaims the resurrection, and confirms the faith

---

[17]Germanus is using the term ἱερεὺς—priest—in its archaic sense, referring to the president of the eucharist, who could at this time be either a bishop or a presbyter. As the liturgy he describes here is that of Hagia Sophia, the cathedral of the capital city of the empire, the celebrant would most likely be a bishop.

ἐν τῷ λίθῳ τοῦ τάφου, ἀποκυλίων τῇ χειρί, δεικνύων τῷ
σχήματι, βοῶν τῇ φωνῇ ἐν τρόμῳ τοῦ διακόνου κηρύττοντος
τὴν τριήμερον ἔγερσιν, ὑφῶν τὸ καταπέτασμα καὶ λέγων·
Στῶμεν καλῶς· ἰδοὺ πρώτη ἡμέρα· στῶμεν μετὰ φόβου· ἰδοὺ
δευτέρα ἡμέρα· ἐν εἰρήνῃ προσφέρειν· ἰδοὺ τρίτη ἡμέρα. Ὁ
λαὸς βοᾷ τὴν τῆς ἀναστάσεως τοῦ Χριστοῦ χάριν· Ἔλεον
εἰρήνης, θυσίαν αἰνέσεως. Ὁ ἱερεὺς διδάσκει τὸν λαὸν τὴν
διὰ τῆς χάριτος θεογνωσίαν τὴν τριαδικήν. Ἡ χάρις τῆς
ἁγίας καὶ ὁμοουσίου Τριάδος μετὰ πάντων ἡμῶν. Ὁ λαὸς
συνομολογεῖ καὶ συνεύχεται καὶ λέγει. Καὶ μετὰ τοῦ Πνεύ-
ματός σου. Εἶτα πάντας ἀναβιβάζων ὁ ἱερεὺς εἰς τὴν ἄνω
Ἱερουσαλὴμ εἰς τὸ ὄρος τὸ ἅγιον αὐτοῦ καὶ βοᾷ· Βλέπετε
ἄνω σχῶμεν τὰς καρδίας· οἱ πάντες διαμαρτύρονται λέγοντες·
Ἔχομεν πρὸς τὸν Κύριον. Ὁ ἱερεὺς· Εὐχαριστήσωμεν τῷ
Κυρίῳ [Ὁ λαὸς συντίθεται λέγων· Ἄξιον καὶ δίκαιον, εὐ-
χαριστηρίους ὕμνους ἀναπέμποντας τῇ ἁγίᾳ Τριάδι ἄνω
ἔχειν τὸ τῆς ψυχῆς ὄμμα ζητοῦντας τὴν κατοικὴν τῆς ἄνω
Ἱερουσαλήμ].

Εἶτα πρόσεισιν ὁ ἱερεὺς μετὰ παρρησίας τῷ θρόνῳ τῆς
χάριτος τοῦ Θεοῦ μετὰ ἀληθινῆς καρδίας ἐν πληροφορίᾳ πίστεως ἀπαγγέλλων τῷ Θεῷ καὶ συλλαλῶν οὐκ ἔτι διὰ νε-
φέλης ὡς ποτὲ Μωϋσῆς ἐν τῇ σκηνῇ τοῦ μαρτυρίου, ἀλλὰ
ἀνακεκαλυμμένῳ προσώπῳ τὴν δόξαν Κυρίου κατοπτεύων·
μεμύηται τὴν τῆς ἁγίας Τριάδος θεογνωσίαν καὶ πίστιν καὶ
μόνος μόνῳ προσλαλεῖ Θεοῦ μυστήρια ἐπαγγέλλων ἐν μυστη-
ρίῳ τὰ κεκρυμμένα πρὸ τῶν αἰώνων καὶ ἀπὸ γενεῶν, νυνὶ
φανερωθέντων ἡμῖν διὰ τῆς ἐπιφανείας τοῦ Υἱοῦ τοῦ Θεοῦ.
Εἴπερ ἡμῖν ἐξηγήσατο ὁ μονογενὴς Υἱὸς ὁ ὢν εἰς τὸν κόλπον
τοῦ Πατρός, καθὼς ἐλάλησεν ὁ Θεὸς τῷ Μωϋσῇ ἀοράτως
καὶ ὁ Μωϋσῆς πρὸς τὸν Θεόν, οὕτως καὶ ὁ ἱερεὺς μέσον τῶν
δύο χερουβὶμ ἑστὼς ἐν τῷ ἱλαστηρίῳ καὶ κατακύπτων διὰ τὴν
ἄστεκτον καὶ ἀθεώρητον τῆς θεότητος δόξαν τε καὶ λαμπρό-
τητα τὴν ἐπουράνιον λατρείαν νοερῶς ὁρῶν καὶ μυεῖται καὶ
τῆς ζωαρχικῆς Τριάδος τὴν ἔλλαμψιν τοῦ μὲν Θεοῦ καὶ
Πατρὸς τὸ ἄναρχον καὶ ἀγέννητον. [τοῦ δὲ Υἱοῦ καὶ Λόγου

in the Holy Trinity. The angel wearing white approaches the stone of the tomb and rolls it away with his hand, pointing with his garment and exclaiming with an awed voice through the deacon, who proclaims the resurrection on the third day, raising the veil and saying: "Let us stand aright"—behold, the first day!—"Let us stand in fear"—behold, the second day!—"Let us offer in peace"—behold, the third day! The people proclaim thanks for the resurrection of Christ: "A mercy of peace, a sacrifice of praise." The priest teaches the people about the threefold knowledge of God which he learned through grace: "The grace of the holy and consubstantial Trinity be with all of you." The people together confess and pray, saying: "And with your spirit." Then the priest, leading everyone into the heavenly Jerusalem, to His holy mountain, exclaims: "Behold, let us lift up our hearts!" Then all declare: "We lift them up unto the Lord!" The priest says: "Let us give thanks unto the Lord." [The people affirm: "It is meet and right" to send up hymns of thanksgiving to the Holy Trinity, to have the eye of the soul seeking the habitation of the heavenly Jerusalem.]

Then the priest goes with confidence to the throne of the grace of God and, with a true heart and in certainty of faith, speaks to God. He converses no longer through a cloud, as once did Moses in the Tabernacle, but with uncovered face seeing the glory of the Lord. He is learned in the divine knowledge of the Holy Trinity and faith, and "one to one" he addresses God, announcing in mystery the mysteries hidden before the ages and from the generations, but which are now revealed to us through the manifestation of the Son of God—(the manifestation) which the only-begotten Son, who is in the bosom of the Father, revealed to us. God truly spoke invisibly to Moses and Moses to God: so now the priest, standing between the two Cherubim in the sanctuary and bowing on account of the dreadful and uncontemplable glory and bright-

τὸ συνάναρχον καὶ ὁμοούσιον καὶ γεννητόν], τοῦ δὲ ʿΑγίου
Πνεύματος τὸ συναΐδιον καὶ ὁμοφυὲς καὶ ἐκπορευτόν· Τριάδα
ἁγίαν κατὰ τὴν τῶν ὑποστάσεων εἴτ᾽ οὖν προσώπων ἀσύγχυ-
τον ἀϊδιότητα, κατὰ δὲ τὴν τῆς φύσεως ἕνωσιν ἀδιαίρετον
καὶ ἀδιάστατον θεότητα καὶ βασιλείαν καὶ δόξαν, καὶ νοερῶς ὁρᾷ καὶ βοᾷ τὴν τῶν σεραφικῶν δυνάμεων καὶ τετρα-
μόρφων ζῴων τρισάγιον δοξολογίαν, τῶν μὲν χερουβὶμ ἐπι-
σκιαζόντων καὶ τῶν σεραφὶμ κεκραγότων, μεθ᾽ ὧν βοᾷ· «Τὸν
ἐπινίκιον ὕμνον ᾄδοντα, βοῶντα, κεκραγότα καὶ λέγοντα».
Εἶτα· ἅγιος, ἅγιος, ἅγιος Κύριος σαβαώθ· τουτέστιν ὁ τρισάγιος καὶ εἷς Θεὸς τῶν δυνάμεων· «ὡσαννὰ ἐν τοῖς ὑψίστοις,
εὐλογημένος ὁ ἐρχόμενος ἐν ὀνόματι Κυρίου». Τὸ ὡσαννά,
ἐστὶ «σῶσον δή, ὡς φῶς, φησίν, ὁ ἐρχόμενος ἐν ὀνόματι
Κυρίου».

ʿΟ δὲ πᾶσι προσφωνούμενος πνευματικὸς ᾽Ασπα-
σμὸς τὴν ἐσομένην πάντων πρὸς ἀλλήλους ἐν τῷ καιρῷ
τῆς τῶν μελλόντων (ἀρρήτων) ἀγαθῶν ἀποκαλύ-
ψεως κατὰ πίστιν τε καὶ ἀγάπην ὁμόνοιάν τε καὶ
ὁμογνωμοσύνην καὶ ταυτότητα λογικήν, δι᾽ ἣν τὴν
πρὸς τὸν Λόγον καὶ Θεὸν οἰκείωσιν οἱ ἄξιοι δέχον-
ται, προτυποῖ καὶ προδιαγράφει· λόγου γὰρ σύμβο-
λον τὸ στόμα καθ᾽ ὃν μάλιστα πᾶσιν ἅπαντες οἱ λόγου
μετειληφότες ὡς λογικοὶ καὶ τῷ πρώτῳ καὶ μόνῳ
Λόγῳ καὶ παντὸς αἰτίῳ λόγου συμφύονται.

ʿΗ δέ... γινομένη Κλεῖσις τῶν θυρῶν τῆς ἁγίας
τοῦ Θεοῦ ἐκκλησίας τήν τε τῶν ὑλικῶν δηλοῖ πάρο-
δον καὶ τὴν γενησομένην μετὰ τὸν φοβερὸν ἐκεῖνον
ἀφορισμὸν καὶ τὴν φοβερωτέραν ψῆφον εἰς τὸν νοη-

ness of the Godhead, and contemplating the heavenly liturgy, is initiated even into the splendor of the life-giving Trinity—of the God and Father, Who is eternal and unbegotten; [of the Son and Word, Who is also without beginning, consubstantial, and begotten]; of the Holy Spirit, Who is co-eternal of the same nature, and proceed-ing—the Holy Trinity which is eternally unconfused in its hypostases, and therefore persons, and which, by the unity of its nature, is the indivisible and inseparable divinity, kingship, and glory. And the priest contemplates and proclaims the thrice-holy glorification of the seraphic powers and of the four-fold creatures. With the over-shadowing Cherubim and the Seraphim who cry aloud, he exclaims: "Singing the triumphant hymn, shouting, pro-claiming, and saying," then "Holy, holy, holy, Lord of Sabaoth"—this is the thrice-holy and one God of the powers—"Hosanna in the highest, blessed is he who comes in the name of the Lord." Hosanna means "save," who, as light, comes in the name of the Lord.

The spiritual salutation, pronounced by all, portrays the future faith, love, concord, unanimity and reasonable identity of everyone for one another through which the worthy receive familiarity to-wards the Word of God. For the symbol of the word is the mouth, by virtue of which almost everyone who participates in the word as a rational being also grows together with the first and only Word and author of every word.[18]

The closing of the doors of the holy church of God materially points to the transition and to the future, after that fearful separation and dread-

---

[18]This paragraph is taken from the *Mystagogy* of Maximus the Confessor, ch 17.

τὸν κόσμον ἤτοι τὸν νυμφῶνα τοῦ Χριστοῦ τῶν ἀξίων εἴσοδον καὶ τὴν ἐν ταῖς αἰσθήσεσι τῆς κατὰ τὴν ἀπάτην ἐνεργείας τελείαν ἀποβολήν.

Ἡ δὲ τοῦ θείου συμβόλου τῆς πίστεως γενομένη παρὰ πάντων ὁμολογία τὴν ἐφ' οἷς ἐσώθημεν παραδόξοις λόγοις τε καὶ τρόποις τῆς πανσόφου περὶ ἡμᾶς τοῦ Θεοῦ προνοίας γενησομένην μυστικὴν εὐχαριστίαν κατὰ τὸν αἰῶνα τὸν μέλλοντα προσημαίνει· δι' ἧς εὐγνώμονας ἐπὶ τῇ θείᾳ εὐεργεσίᾳ ἑαυτοὺς συνιστῶσιν οἱ ἄξιοι· πλὴν ταύτης τῶν περὶ αὐτοὺς ἀπείρων θείων ἀγαθῶν ἀντεισαγαγεῖν ἄλλο τι καθ' ὁτιοῦν οὐκ ἔχοντες.

Τὰ δὲ ῥιπίδια καὶ οἱ διάκονοι ἐμφαίνουσι τὰ ἐξαπτέρυγα σεραφὶμ καὶ τὴν τῶν πολυομμάτων χερουβὶμ ἐμφέρειαν· καὶ γὰρ κατὰ τὴν οὐράνιον καὶ ὑπερκόσμιον καὶ νοερὰν ὄντως τάξιν οὕτως καὶ τὰ ἐπίγεια μιμοῦνται. Καὶ γὰρ τετράμορφα ζῶα ἀντιφωνητικῶς ἀλλήλοις ἀντιδεχόμενα τὸ μὲν Α' (πρῶτον), τὸ ὡς ὁμοίωμα λέοντος, βοᾷ ΑΓΙΟΣ· τὸ Β' (δεύτερον), τὸ ὡς ὁμοίωμα μόσχου, βοᾷ ΑΓΙΟΣ· τὸ δὲ τρίτον (Γ'), τὸ ὡς ὁμοίωμα ἀνθρώπου, βοᾷ ΑΓΙΟΣ· τὸ δὲ Δ' (τέταρτον), ὡς ὁμοίωμα ἀετοῦ, βοᾷ ΚΥΡΙΟΣ ΣΑΒΑΩΘ· ἐν τρισὶν ἁγιασμοῖς εἰς μίαν συνιοῦσι κυριότητα καὶ δύναμιν καὶ θεότητα καθὼς ὁ προφήτης Ἡσαΐας τεθέαται ὅτε εἶδε τὸν Κύριον ἐπὶ θρόνου ὑψηλοῦ καὶ ἐπηρμένου, καὶ τὰς σεραφικὰς δυνάμεις κύκλῳ ἑστώσας καὶ ἐκ τῆς φωνῆς ἐπλήσθη ὁ οἶκος καπνοῦ. Τὸ δὲ «ἀπεστάλη ἓν τῶν σεραφὶμ καὶ ἔλαβεν ἄνθρακα ἐν τῇ χειρὶ ὃν τῇ λαβίδι ἔλαβεν ἀπὸ τοῦ θυσιαστηρίου», σημαίνει τὸν ἱερέα καὶ αὐτὸν κατέχοντα τὸν νοερὸν ἄνθρακα Χριστὸν τῇ λαβίδι τῆς χειρὸς αὐτοῦ ἐν τῷ

ful sentence in the spiritual world, that is, the entrance of the worthy into the bridal chamber of Christ and the final rejection of the deceptive operation of the senses.[19]

Further, the profession of the divine symbol of faith, which is made by all, prefigures the mystical thanksgiving of the future age because of the wonderful words and ways of the providence of the all-wise God for us, by which we are saved. By this thanksgiving, those who offer in gratitude for the divine benefits on their behalf constitute the worthy: but they have nothing to give in return for the boundless divine goods on their behalf.[20]

The fans and the deacons are in the likeness of the six-winged Seraphim and the many-eyed Cherubim, for in this way earthly things imitate the heavenly, transcendent, the spiritual order of things. And to one another the four-formed creatures[21] antiphonally exclaim: the first, in the likeness of a lion, cries out "Holy"; the second, in the likeness of a calf, cries out "Holy"; the third, in the likeness of a man, cries out "Holy"; and the fourth, in the likeness of an eagle, cries out "Lord of Sabaoth." In the three acclamations, they perceive one lordship, power, and divinity, as the Prophet Isaiah beheld when he saw the Lord on a lofty and exalted throne and the seraphic powers standing around, and the house was filled with smoke from their vocie (cf Is 6:1-4). And "One of the seraphim was sent, and he took into his hand a coal which he had taken from the altar with a pair of tongs" (Is 6:6)—this represents the priest who with the tongs

---

[19]*Ibid.*, ch. 15.
[20]*Ibid.*, ch. 18.
[21]The beast of the Apocalypse. See the note in ch 32.

ἁγίῳ (θυσιαστηρίῳ), καὶ ἁγιάζοντα καὶ καθαίροντα (τοὺς δεχομένους) καὶ μεταλαμβάνοντας. Καὶ γὰρ «εἰς οὐράνια καὶ ἀχειροποίητα ἅγια εἰσῆλθεν ὁ Χριστὸς καὶ ἐνεφανίσθη ἐν δόξῃ τῷ προσώπῳ τοῦ Θεοῦ ὑπὲρ ἡμῶν γενόμενος ἀρχιερεὺς μέγας διεληλυθὼς τοὺς οὐρανούς, καὶ ἔχομεν αὐτὸν παράκλητον πρὸς τὸν Πατέρα καὶ ἱλασμὸν ὑπὲρ τῶν ἁμαρτιῶν ἡμῶν»· ὃς καταρτισάμενος ἡμῖν τὸ ἅγιον καὶ ἀΐδιον αὐτοῦ σῶμα, λύτρον ὑπὲρ πάντων ἡμῶν, καθὼς αὐτὸς λέγει· «Πάτερ ἁγίασον αὐτοὺς ἐν ὀνόματί σου οὓς δέδωκάς μοι, ἵνα ὦσι αὐτοὶ ἡγιασμένοι», καὶ «θέλω ἵνα ὦσι ὅπου ἐγώ εἰμι καὶ θεωρῶσι τὴν δόξαν τὴν ἐμὴν ὅτι ἠγάπησας αὐτοὺς καθὰ ἠγάπησας ἐμὲ πρὸ καταβολῆς κόσμου».

Εἶτα πάλιν ὁ ἱερεὺς ἀπαγγέλλει τῷ Θεῷ καὶ Πατρὶ τὰ τῆς Χριστοῦ ἐνανθρωπήσεως μυστήρια, τὴν ἐξ ἁγίας Παρθένου καὶ θεοτόκου ἀνέκφραστον καὶ ἔνδοξον γέννησιν, τὴν ἀναστροφὴν καὶ πολίτευσιν ἐν τῷ κόσμῳ, τὸν σταυρόν, τὸν θάνατον καὶ τὴν τῶν δεσμίων ψυχῶν ἐλευθερίαν, τὴν ἐκ νεκρῶν αὐτοῦ τριήμερον καὶ ἁγίαν ἀνάστασιν, τὴν ἐν τοῖς οὐρανοῖς ἀνάληψιν, τὴν ἐκ δεξιῶν τοῦ Θεοῦ καὶ Πατρὸς καθέδραν, τὴν δευτέραν καὶ μέλλουσαν αὐτοῦ ἔνδοξον παρουσίαν πάλιν πρὸς ἡμᾶς. Καὶ μυσταγωγεῖται γαστέρα πρὸ ἑωσφώρου Θεὸν ἀγέννητον, τουτέστι τὸν Θεὸν καὶ Πατέρα, καὶ πρὸ αἰώνων τὸν Θεὸν γεννῶσαν καθὼς λέγει· «ἐκ γαστρὸς πρὸ ἑωσφόρου ἐγέννησά σε»· ὅνπερ καὶ παρακαλεῖ πάλιν τελειῶσαι τὸ μυστήριον τοῦ Υἱοῦ αὐτοῦ καὶ γενηθῆναι, ἤτοι μεταποιηθῆναι τὸν ἄρτον καὶ τὸν οἶνον εἰς σῶμα καὶ αἷμα αὐτοῦ τοῦ Χριστοῦ καὶ Θεοῦ· καὶ πληρωθήσεται τό· «Ἐγὼ σήμερον γεγέννηκά σε». Ὅθεν καὶ τὸ Πνεῦμα τὸ Ἅγιον τῇ εὐδοκίᾳ τοῦ Πατρὸς καὶ βουλήσει ἀοράτως παρὸν ὑποδεικνύει τὴν θείαν ἐνέργειαν· καὶ τῇ χειρὶ τοῦ ἱερέως ἐπι-

ON THE DIVINE LITURGY

(his hands) holds in the holy altar the spiritual coal, Christ, Who santifies and purifies those who receive and partake. For Christ has entered the heavenly sanctuary not made with hands (cf Hb 9:24), and He has appeared in glory in the presence of God on our behalf, having become a great high priest (cf Hb 6:20) who has penetrated the heavens (cf Hb 4:14); and we have Him as an advocate before the Father, and as the expiation for our sins (cf I Jn 2:1-2). He gave us His holy and eternal body in ransom for all of us, as He says: "Father, sanctify them, whom you gave me in your name, so that they may be sanctified" (cf Jn 17:11, 17, 19); and "I desire that they may be where I am, and that they might behold my glory, because you loved them as you loved me before the foundation of the world" (cf Jn 17:24).

Then again the priest declares to the God and Father the mysteries of Christ's incarnation, His ineffable and glorious birth from the holy Virgin Theotokos, His dwelling and life in the world, the cross, the death, the liberation of the souls in bondage, His holy resurrection from the dead on the third day, His ascension into heaven, His sitting at the right hand of the God and Father, His second and future glorious coming again to us. And the priest expounds on the unbegotten God, that is the God and Father, and on the womb which bore the Son before the morning star and before the ages. as it is written: "Out of the womb before the morning star have I begotten you" (Ps 109:3). And again the priest asks God to accomplish and bring about the mystery of His Son— that is, that the bread and wine be changed into the body and blood of Christ God—so that it might be fulfilled that "Today I have begotten you" (Ps 2:7). Then the Holy Spirit, invisibly present by the good will and volition of the Father, demonstrates the divine operation and, by the hand of the priest, testifies, completes, and changes

μαρτυρεῖ καὶ ἐπισφραγίζει καὶ τελειοῖ τὰ προκείμενα ἅγια δῶρα εἰς σῶμα καὶ αἷμα Ἰησοῦ Χριστοῦ τοῦ Κυρίου ἡμῶν τοῦ εἰπόντος· ὅτι «ὑπὲρ αὐτῶν ἐγὼ ἁγιάζω ἐμαυτόν, ἵνα ὦσι καὶ αὐτοὶ ἡγιασμένοι· ὅπως ὁ τρώγων μου τὴν σάρκα καὶ πίνων μου τὸ αἷμα, ἐν ἐμοὶ μένει κἀγὼ ἐν αὐτῷ». Ὅθεν γενόμενοι τῶν θείων μυστηρίων αὐτόπται καὶ μέτοχοι ζωῆς ἀθανάτου καὶ κοινωνοὶ θείας φύσεως, δοξάσωμεν τὸ μέγα καὶ ἀκατάληπτον καὶ ἀνεξιχνίαστον μυστήριον τῆς οἰκονομίας Χριστοῦ καὶ Θεοῦ· ὅθεν καὶ δοξάζοντες βοῶμεν· «Σὲ ὑμνοῦμεν» τὸν Θεὸν καὶ Πατέρα· «σὲ εὐλογοῦμεν» τὸν Υἱὸν καὶ Λόγον· «σοὶ εὐχαριστοῦμεν» τῷ Ἁγίῳ Πνεύματι· «Κύριε ὁ Θεὸς ἡμῶν», Τριὰς γὰρ ἐν μονάδι ὁμοούσιος καὶ ἀδιαίρετος, παράδοξον ἔχουσα καὶ τὴν διαίρεσιν τῶν προσώπων καὶ τὴν ἕνωσιν τῆς μιᾶς φύσεως καὶ θεότητος· καὶ γὰρ τὸ ἐπικεκυφότως ποιεῖν τὸν ἱερέα τὴν θείαν μυσταγωγείαν ἐμφαίνει τὸ συλλαλεῖν ἀοράτως τῷ μόνῳ Θεῷ. Ὅθεν καὶ τὴν θείαν φωτοφάνειαν ὁρᾷ, καὶ τῇ λαμπρότητι τῆς δόξης τοῦ προσώπου τοῦ Θεοῦ ἐκφαιδρύνεται καὶ ὑποστέλλει ἑαυτῷ τῷ φόβῳ καὶ τῇ αἰδοῖ· καθὼς Μωϋσῆς ὅτε εἶδε τὸν Θεὸν ἐν εἴδει πυρὸς ἐν τῷ ὄρει ἔντρομος γενόμενος ἀνέστρεφε καὶ ἐκάλυψε τὸ πρόσωπον· εὐλαβεῖτο γὰρ κατανοῆσαι ἀπὸ τῆς δόξης τοῦ προσώπου, φησί.

Γίνεται δὲ καὶ ἡ μνήμη τῶν κεκοιμημένων πρὸς τὸν Θεὸν τῶν πνευμάτων καὶ πάσης σαρκός, τὸν καὶ νεκρῶν καὶ ζώντων τὴν κυρίαν ἔχοντα καὶ δεσπόζοντα τῶν ἐπουρανίων καὶ ἐπιγείων καὶ καταχθονίων· καὶ ὡς τοῦ βασιλέως Χριστοῦ παρόντος, καὶ τοῦ Ἁγίου Πνεύματος πάντας προσκαλουμένου ζῶντας καὶ μεταστάντας πρὸς τὰς ἐκεῖθεν μονὰς καὶ καταπαύσεις· εἰς τὴν τοῦ Θεοῦ καὶ Κυρίου καὶ Σωτῆρος ἡμῶν Ἰησοῦ Χριστοῦ προέλευσιν, συναθροισθῆναι

the holy gifts which are set forth into the body and blood of Jesus Christ our Lord, Who says: "For their sake I sanctify myself, that they also may be sanctified" (Jn 17:19), so that "He who eats my flesh and drinks my blood abides in me and I in him" (Jn 6:56). Thus becoming eye-witnesses of the mysteries of God, partakers of eternal life, and sharers in divine nature, let us glorify the great, immeasurable, and unsearchable mystery of the dispensa-tion of Christ God, and glorifying Him let us cry: "We praise you"—the God and Father—"We bless you"—the Son and Word—"We give thanks to you"—the Holy Spirit—"O Lord our God"—the Trinity in unity consub-stantial and undivided, marvellously possessing both the distinction of persons and the unity of the one nature and divinity. The priest's performing the divine mystery while bowing down manifests that he converses invisibly with the only God: for he sees the divine illumination, he is made radiant by the brightness of the glory of the face of God, and he recoils in fear and shame like Moses, who, when he saw God in the form of fire on the mountain, trembled, turned away, and covered his face, fearing to contemplate the glory of God's face.

Then comes the remembrance of those who have fallen asleep in the God of spirits and of all flesh, Who is the Lord of both the dead and the living, and Who rules over those in heaven, on earth, and in the lower regions. For Christ the King is present, and the Holy Spirit calls all the living and the dead to unity and rest until the appearance of our God and Lord and Savior Jesus Christ and to assemble and come before His face; because the chains of all the souls in Hades have been loosed through the death and resurrection of Christ. For He has been raised from the dead, having become the first-fruit and first-born from the dead (cf I Cor 15:20). He prepared a way for all to the resurrection from the dead and granted

καὶ προφθάσαι τὸ πρόσωπον αὐτοῦ ὡς πάντων τῶν ἐν Ἅδου ψυχῶν ἀπολυθέντων δεσμῶν, διὰ τοῦ θανάτου καὶ τῆς ἀναστάσεως Χριστοῦ· αὐτὸς γὰρ «ἐγήγερται ἐκ νεκρῶν, ἀπαρχὴ καὶ πρωτότοκος τῶν κεκοιμημένων γενόμενος»· καὶ πᾶσιν ὁδοποιήσας τὴν ἐκ νεκρῶν ἀνάστασιν, καὶ πρὸς τὴν ἀθάνατον καὶ μακαρίαν ζωὴν ἀναπαύων τοὺς ἐπ᾽ ἐλπίδι τῆς ἐγέρσεως αὐτοῦ κεκοιμημένους· καὶ συγκαλοῦνται μετὰ προφητῶν καὶ ἀποστόλων καὶ ἱεραρχῶν τῶν χριστιανῶν αἱ ψυχαὶ συνελθεῖν καὶ ἀνακλιθῆναι μετὰ Ἀβραὰμ καὶ Ἰσαὰκ καὶ Ἰακὼβ ἐν τῇ μυστικῇ τραπέζῃ τῆς βασιλείας Χριστοῦ.

Ὅθεν εἰς ἑνότητα πίστεως, καὶ κοινωνίαν Πνεύματος ἐλθόντες διὰ τῆς οἰκονομίας τοῦ ὑπὲρ ἡμῶν ἀποθανόντος καὶ καθίσαντος ἐν δεξιᾷ τοῦ Πατρὸς οὐκ ἔτι ἐπὶ γῆς ἐσμεν, ἀλλ᾽ ἐν τῷ θρόνῳ τοῦ Θεοῦ τῷ βασιλικῷ παρεστηκότες· ἐν οὐρανῷ ὅπου ὁ Χριστός ἐστι καθὼς αὐτὸς λέγει, ὅτι «Πάτερ δίκαιε, ἁγίασον αὐτοὺς ἐν τῷ ὀνόματί σου οὓς δέδωκάς μοι, ἵνα ὅπου εἰμὶ ἐγὼ κἀκεῖνοι ὦσι μετ᾽ ἐμοῦ». Τοίνυν «τὴν υἱοθεσίαν ἀπολαβόντες καὶ συγκληρονόμοι τοῦ Χριστοῦ γενόμενοι διὰ τῆς χάριτος αὐτοῦ καὶ οὐκ ἐξ ἔργων», ἔχομεν τὸ πνεῦμα τοῦ Υἱοῦ τοῦ Θεοῦ, οὗτινος τὴν ἐνέργειαν καὶ τὴν χάριν θεωρῶν ὁ ἱερεὺς βοᾷ καὶ λέγει· Ἀββᾶ ὁ Πατὴρ ὁ οὐράνιος, ἀξίωσον ἡμᾶς, μετὰ παρρησίας τολμᾶν ἀκατακρίτως καὶ λέγειν·

ΕΞΗΓΗΣΙΣ ΕΙΣ ΤΟ ΠΑΤΕΡ ΗΜΩΝ

42. ΠΑΤΕΡ ΗΜΩΝ, Ο ΕΝ ΤΟΙΣ ΟΥΡΑΝΟΙΣ, ΑΓΙΑΣΘΗΤΩ ΤΟ ΟΝΟΜΑ ΣΟΥ· τὸ ὄνομά ἐστιν τοῦ Υἱοῦ τοῦ Θεοῦ.

ΠΑΤΕΡ δὲ εἰπὼν δείκνυσί σοι τίνων ἀγαθῶν ἠξιώθης, υἱός γε Θεοῦ γεγονώς· ἐν δὲ τῷ εἰπεῖν ΕΝ ΟΥΡΑΝΟΙΣ, ἔδειξε τὴν πατρίδα καὶ τὸν οἶκον τοῦ Πατρός σου, ἐὰν γὰρ θέλεις ἔχειν πατέρα τὸν Θεόν, πρὸς τὸν οὐρανὸν βλέπε καὶ μὴ

rest in eternal and blessed life to those who have fallen asleep in the hope of His resurrection. The souls of Christians are called together to assemble with the prophets, apostles, and hierarchs in order to recline with Abraham, Isaac, and Jacob at the mystical banquet of the Kingdom of Christ.

Thereby having come into the unity of faith and communion of the Spirit through the dispensation of the One who died for us and is sitting at the right hand of the Father, we are no longer on earth but standing by the royal throne of God in heaven, where Christ is, just as He himself says: "Righteous Father, sanctify in your name those whom you gave me, so that where I am, they may be with me" (cf Jn 17). Therefore, receiving adoption and becoming co-heirs with Christ through His grace, and not through works, we have the spirit of the Son of God. Contemplating His power and grace, the priest calls out, saying: "Abba, heavenly Father, make us worthy to say boldly and without condemnation:"

EXPLANATION OF THE OUR FATHER

42. OUR FATHER, WHO ART IN HEAVEN, HALLOWED BE YOUR NAME: the name is that of the Son of God.

Saying "Father" points out to you of whose goods you have been made worthy, now that you have become a son of God. Saying "in heaven" points out your Father's native country and home: if you want to have God as a father, look to heaven and not to earth. For you do not

πρὸς τὴν γῆν. Οὐ λέγεις δὲ ΠΑΤΕΡ ΜΟΥ ἀλλὰ ΠΑΤΕΡ ΗΜΩΝ ὡσὰν ἔχεις πάντας ὡς ἀδελφοὺς ἑνὸς Πατρός.

ΑΓΙΑΣΘΗΤΩ ΤΟ ΟΝΟΜΑ ΣΟΥ τουτέστι, ποίησον ἡμᾶς ἁγίους ἵνα σὺ δι᾿ ἡμᾶς δοξάζῃ· ὡς γὰρ 6λασφημεῖται δι᾿ ἐμοῦ ὁ Θεός, οὕτω δοξάζεται δι᾿ ἐμέ.

ΕΛΘΕΤΩ Η ΒΑΣΙΛΕΙΑ ΣΟΥ τουτέστιν, ἡ δευτέρα παρουσία· ὁ γὰρ συνειδὸς ἀγαθὸν ἔχων πεπαρρησιασμένος εὔχεται ἐλθεῖν τὴν ἀνάστασιν καὶ τὴν κρίσιν.

ΓΕΝΗΘΗΤΩ ΤΟ ΘΕΛΗΜΑ ΣΟΥ ΩΣ ΕΝ ΟΥΡΑΝΩ ΚΑΙ ΕΠΙ ΤΗΣ ΓΗΣ· ὥσπερ, φησίν, οἱ ἄγγελοι ποιοῦσι τὸ θέλημά σου, οὕτω καὶ ἡμᾶς δὸς ποιεῖν αὐτό.

ΤΟΝ ΑΡΤΟΝ ΗΜΩΝ ΤΟΝ ΕΠΙΟΥΣΙΟΝ ΔΟΣ ΗΜΙΝ ΣΗΜΕΡΟΝ· ἐπιούσιον, τὸν ἐπὶ τῇ οὐσίᾳ ἡμῶν καὶ συστάσει ἀρκοῦντα φησίν· ἀναιρεῖ δὲ περὶ τὴν αὔριον μέριμναν. Καὶ τὸ σῶμα δὲ τοῦ Χριστοῦ ἄρτος ἐστὶν ἐπιούσιος· οὗ μεταλαμβάνειν ἀκρίτως εὐχόμεθα·

ΚΑΙ ΑΦΕΣ ΗΜΙΝ ΤΟ ΟΦΕΙΛΗΜΑΤΑ ΗΜΩΝ, ΩΣ ΚΑΙ ΗΜΕΙΣ ΑΦΙΕΜΕΝ ΤΟΙΣ ΟΦΕΙΛΕΤΑΙΣ ΗΜΩΝ· ἐπεὶ καὶ μετὰ τὸ βάπτισμα ἁμαρτάνομεν, ἱκετεύομεν ἵνα ἀφήσῃ ἡμῖν τὰ χρέη ἡμῶν ἐὰν ἡμεῖς μὴ μνησικακῶμεν· ἐμὲ γὰρ ἔχει ὁ Θεὸς παράδειγμα, καὶ ὃ ποιῶ ἐπ᾿ ἄλλῳ, ποιεῖ ἐπ᾿ ἐμέ.

ΚΑΙ ΜΗ ΕΙΣΕΝΕΓΚΗΣ ΗΜΑΣ ΕΙΣ ΠΕΙΡΑΣΜΟΝ· ἀσθενεῖς ἐσμεν οἱ ἄνθρωποι· διὸ οὐ δεῖ περιπίπτειν αὐτοὺς εἰς πειρασμούς, ἀλλ᾿ εὔχεσθαι μὴ καταποθῆναι ὑπὸ τοῦ πειρασμοῦ· ὁ γὰρ καταποθεὶς καὶ νικηθεὶς ἐκεῖνος εἰσενέχθη εἰς τὸν βόθρον τοῦ πειρασμοῦ· ἀλλ᾿ ὁ ἐμπεσὼν μέν, νικήσας δέ;

ΑΛΛΑ ΡΥΣΑΙ ΗΜΑΣ ΑΠΟ ΤΟΥ ΠΟΝΗΡΟΥ· οὐκ εἶπεν ἀπὸ τῶν πονηρῶν ἀνθρώπων, οὐ γὰρ ἀδικοῦσιν ἡμᾶς, ἀλλ᾿ ὁ ΠΟΝΗΡΟΣ:—

say "my Father," but "our Father," since you have all men as brothers of the one Father.

HALLOWED BE YOUR NAME, that is, make us holy so that You may be glorified by us. For as God is blasphemed by me, so He is also glorified by me.

YOUR KINGDOM COME, that is, the second coming: for he who has a good conscience boldly desires the coming of the resurrection and the judgment.

YOUR WILL BE DONE, ON EARTH AS IN HEAVEN—just as, it says, the angels do Your will, so grant that we may do it.

GIVE US THIS DAY OUR DAILY BREAD—it means the bread which is sufficient for our nature and existence. He removes the care for the morrow. The body of Christ is the daily bread, and we pray that we may share in it blamelessly.

AND FORGIVE US OUR TRESPASSES, AS WE FORGIVE THOSE WHO TRESPASS AGAINST US, because we sin even after baptism. We pray that He might forgive us our debts if we do bear a grudge: for God has me as an example, and what I do to the other, He does unto me.

AND LEAD US NOT INTO TEMPTATION. We men are weak; therefore, it does not behoove us to fall into temptation, but rather to pray not to be overwhelmed by temptation. For he who is overwhelmed and overcome is led into the pit of temptation: but he who has fallen, has he prevailed?

BUT DELIVER US FROM THE EVIL ONE. He does not say "from evil men," for they do not wrong us, but "the Evil One."

Ἡ δὲ παναγία τε καὶ σεπτὴ τοῦ μεγάλου καὶ
μακαρίου Θεοῦ (καὶ Πατρὸς) ἐπίκλησις τῆς δοθη-
σομένης ἐνυποστάτου τε καὶ ἐνυπάρκτου κατὰ δωρεὰν
καὶ χάριν τοῦ Ἁγίου Πνεύματος υἱοθεσίας ἐστὶ σύμ-
βολον· καθ᾽ ἥν, πάσης ὑπερνικωμένης τε καὶ καλυ-
πτομένης ἀνθρωπίνης ἰδιότητος τῇ ἐπιφοιτήσει τῆς
χάριτος, υἱοὶ Θεοῦ χρηματίσουσί τε καὶ ἔσονται πάντες οἱ ἅγιοι, ὅσοι (δι᾽ ἀρετῶν) ἀπεντεῦθεν ἤδη τῷ
θείῳ τῆς ἀγαθότητος κάλλει ἑαυτοὺς λαμπρῶς τε καὶ
ἐπιδόξως ἐφαίδρυναν.

43. Εἶτα ὁ ἱερεὺς βοᾷ τοῖς πᾶσι λέγων· ὅτι ἐγὼ ἄν-
θρωπός εἰμι ὁμοιοπαθὴς ὑμῖν καὶ οὐ γινώσκω τὰ ἑκάστου
ὑμῶν πλημμελήματα· βλέπετε, θεωρεῖτε· ἰδοὺ ὁ Θεός· καὶ
Θεός ἐστιν ὁ ἅγιος ἐν ἁγίοις ἀναπαυόμενος. Ὁ λαὸς ὁμολογεῖ καὶ λέγει· «Εἷς ἅγιος, εἷς κύριος ἡμῶν Ἰησοῦς Χριστὸς»
σὺν Θεῷ καὶ Πατρὶ καὶ Ἁγίῳ Πνεύματι. Καὶ ὁ μὲν Μωϋσῆς
τὸ «αἷμα ἐρράντισε τῶν τράγων, καὶ τῶν μόσχων, τῷ λαῷ
λέγων· τοῦτο τὸ αἷμα τῆς διαθήκης» τοῦ Θεοῦ ἐστιν· ὁ δὲ
Χριστὸς καὶ Θεὸς τὸ ἴδιον σῶμα ἔδωκε καὶ τὸ ἴδιον αἷμα
ἐξέχεε καὶ ἐκέρασε, τὸ τῆς καινῆς διαθήκης, λέγων· Τοῦτο
ἐστὶ τὸ σῶμά μου καὶ τὸ αἷμά μου· τὸ κλώμενον καὶ διαρραν-
τιζόμενον εἰς ἄφεσιν ἁμαρτιῶν. Καὶ οὕτω λοιπὸν μετὰ τοι-
αύτης εὐνοίας, ἐσθίομεν τὸν ἄρτον καὶ πίνομεν τὸ ποτήριον,
ὡς σῶμα καὶ αἷμα τοῦ Θεοῦ, τὸν θάνατον καὶ τὴν ἀνάστασιν
ὁμολογοῦντες τοῦ Κυρίου Ἰησοῦ Χριστοῦ, ᾧ ἡ δόξα εἰς
τοὺς αἰῶνας ἀμήν.—

Ἡ δὲ κατὰ τὸ τέλος τῆς μυστικῆς ἱερουργίας
παρὰ παντὸς τοῦ λαοῦ γινομένη τοῦ Εἷς ἅγιος καὶ
τῶν ἐξῆς ὁμολογία, τὴν ὑπὲρ λόγον καὶ νοῦν πρὸς
τὸ ἓν τῆς θείας ἁπλότητος κρύφιον γενησομένην τῶν

The all-holy and sacred invocation of the great and blessed God (and Father) is a symbol of the subsistent and existing sonship which has been bestowed according to the gift and grace of the Holy Spirit. According to this adoption, when all human distinctiveness is surpassed and covered by the visitation of grace, they are called sons of God and they all will be saints, as many as (through gracious acts) thenceforth have splendidly and gloriously cleansed themselves by the divine beauty of goodness.[22]

43. Then the priest exclaims, saying to all: I am a man of like passions with you, and I do not know the sins of each of you. "Look, see, behold God!" And "God is the Holy One who abides in the saints." The people respond, saying: "One is holy, one is our Lord, Jesus Christ," with the God and Father and the Holy Spirit. For in the past Moses sprinkled the blood of the calves and the goats, saying to the people: "This is the blood of the covenant of God." But now the Christ and God has given His own body and poured out and mixed His own blood (cf Hb 9:19 ff), that of the new covenant, saying: "This is my body and my blood, which is broken and poured out for the remission of sins." So henceforth with this understanding we eat the bread and drink the cup, as the body and blood of God, professing the death and resurrection of the Lord Jesus Christ, to whom be glory unto the ages. Amen.

The confession made by all the people near the end of the liturgy—"One is holy," etc.—signifies the future gathering and unity, beyond reason and understanding, of those who have been mys-

---

[22]Extract from Maximus the Confessor, *Mystagogy,* ch 20.

μυστικῶς τε καὶ σοφῶς κατὰ Θεὸν τετελεσμένων συναγωγήν τε καὶ ἕνωσιν δηλοῖ ἐν τῷ ἀγθάρτῳ τῶν νοητῶν αἰῶνι, καθ᾿ ὃν τῆς ἀφανοῦς καὶ ὑπεραρρήτου δόξης τὸ φῶς ἐνοπτεύοντες τῆς μακαρίας μετὰ τῶν ἄνω δυνάμεων, καὶ αὐτοὶ δεκτικοὶ γίνονται καθαρότητος.

Μεθ᾿ ἣν ὡς τέλος πάντων ἡ τῶν μυστηρίων ἡ μετάδοσις γίνεται, μεταποιοῦσα πρὸς ἑαυτὴν καὶ ὁμοίους τῷ κατ᾿ αἰτίαν ἀγαθῷ κατὰ χάριν καὶ μέθεξιν ἀποφαίνουσα τοὺς ἀξίως μεταλαμβάνοντας, ἐν μηδενὶ αὐτοῦ λειπομένους κατὰ τὸ (ἐφικτὸν) ἀνθρώποις (καὶ) ἐνδεχόμενον ὥστε καὶ αὐτοὺς δύνασθαι εἶναί τε καὶ καλεῖσθαι θέσει κατὰ τὴν χάριν θεούς, διὰ τὸν αὐτοὺς ὅλον Θεὸν καὶ μηδὲν αὐτῶν τῆς αὐτοῦ παρουσίας κενὸν καταλείψαντα.

Κοινωνία κέκληται ἡ τῶν θείων μυστηρίων μετάληψις διὰ τὸ τὴν πρὸς Χριστὸν ἡμῖν χαρίζεσθαι ἕνωσιν καὶ κοινωνοὺς ἡμᾶς τῆς αὐτοῦ ποιεῖν βασιλείας.

tically and wisely fulfilled by God, with the hidden one of the divine simplicity, in the incorruptibility of the spiritual age, during which they gaze with the heavenly powers upon the light of the invisible and ineffable glory, which is blessed, and they become capable of becoming pure.

After this, as the conclusion, the distribution of the mysteries takes place, which transforms into itself and makes those who worthily participate similar to the original good by grace, making them in no way deficient, inasmuch as it is accessible and possible for men, so that they too may be able to be and to be called gods by adoption through grace, because the whole God is theirs, and nothing in them is devoid of His presence.[23]

Partaking of the divine mysteries is called Communion because it bestows on us unity with Christ and makes us partakers of His Kingdom.[24]

---

[23]These two paragraphs are extracts from Maximus the Confessor, *Mystagogy*, ch 21.

[24]Extract from Letter I, 228, of Isidore of Pelusium.